The Life and Ti

Charles Masefield, MC.

By

Graham Bebbington

Copyright Graham Bebbington

North Staffordshire Press
Stoke-on-Trent
Staffordshire

The Life and Times of
Charles Masefield MC.

All Rights Reserved

No part of this book may be reproduced in any form by photocopying or any electronic or mechanical means, including information storage and retrieval systems, without permission in writing from both the copyright owner and the publisher of this book.

ISBN 978-0-9928305-3-3

First Published in 2014
Reprinted 2014

By

North Staffordshire Press

Staffordshire University

Business Village

72 Leek Road

Stoke-on-Trent

Staffordshire

United Kingdom

ALSO BY THE SAME AUTHOR:

The Loggerheads Project
(Newcastle Borough Council)

Pit Boy to Prime Minister
(University of Keele)

A Brief Life
(Isle of Wight County Press)

Trentham at War
(Churnet Valley)

Ship Without Water
(Churnet Valley)

The Fledglings
(Churnet Valley)

Trentham Reflections
(Churnet Valley)

Silverdale – The Five Road Ends
(Churnet Valley)

'Humbly, O England, we offer what is of little worth,
Just our bodies and souls and everything else we have;
But thou with thy holy cause wilt hallow our common earth,
Giving us strength in the battle - and peace, if need, in the grave.'

From 'Enlisted' by Charles J. B. Masefield

CONTENTS

                                        Page No.

Acknowledgements		vii
Foreword		xi
Introduction		1
Chapter 1	Born In Pugin Land	3
Chapter 2	Halcyon Days At 'Rosehill'	15
Chapter 3	Schooldays	23
Chapter 4	The Legal Profession And Literary Connections	41
Chapter 5	Return to Cheadle	59
Chapter 6	War - Opening Moves	71
Chapter 7	Enlisted	87
Chapter 8	The Bullring And The Trenches	109
Chapter 9	Special Leave	133
Chapter 10	Retreat Of The Boche	151
Chapter 11	Attack At Dawn!	163
Chapter 12	A Period Of Uncertainty	179
Chapter 13	Letters Of Farewell	193
Chapter 14	Victory Achieved… Another Battle Begins	203
Chapter 15	Epilogue	219
About the Author		227

ACKNOWLEDGEMENTS

My grateful thanks are due to Sarah Elsom for writing the Foreword to the book.

Writing this biography would have been so much harder but for the kind co-operation and assistance of the Masefield family, who generously provided me with copies of correspondence, photographs and other material.

I am also deeply indebted to Professor Christine King CBE (Vice-Chancellor Emeritus, Staffordshire University) for her encouragement, advice and making valuable suggestions at the manuscript stage.

In addition to those quoted in the text or source notes, I am most appreciative of the assistance of the following:-

Mrs P. Piers-Leake; Michael & Fiona Collis; George Short; Mark Offord; Ian Hislop; Richard A.Durrant; John H. Emery; Alan Scott; E.F Malet de Carteret and the Editors & staff of the Sentinel and The Cheadle & Tean Times.

Gratitude is also expressed to Chris Copp (Senior

Museums Officer, Staffordshire County Council); Mrs Delyth Copp (Curator, Newcastle Borough Museum); Mrs D. M. A. Randall (former Head of Archives, Staffordshire County Council); Major Jim Massey & Jeffrey Elson (The Staffordshire Regiment Museum); The Imperial War Museum; Clare George (The British Postal Museum); Sefton Council; Paul L. Stevens (Librarian & Archivist, Repton School); Dr Rainer-Maria Kiel (Bayreuth University); The British Library; and the librarians & staff of Mablethorpe, Scarborough, Lincoln, Grantham, Malvern, Stoke-on-Trent City Central, & Southport libraries. Special thanks are also due to Cathryn Walters, Julie Knapper & Neil Fox at Trentham Library.

Special thanks are also given to John Grindey for his superb cover design.

Finally, my wife Lynne Margaret, as usual, shared in all the pleasures and pain of research and assisted with everything from IT consultancy to being my soundboard throughout the period that research has been ongoing.

Every endeavour has been made to trace source material. If, inadvertently, any copyright has been infringed, the author offers his apology and will correct omissions in any subsequent edition.

Charles J.B Masefield

FOREWORD

I first came across Charles Masefield when, as Curator of the Staffordshire Regiment Museum, I was doing the research for an exhibition on Art and Poetry in the First World War. In the Regimental Archives I came across a rather battered copy of the Poems of Charles Masefield, published in 1919 after his untimely death on the Western Front.

Reading through the small volume it became obvious that here was someone who was beginning to mature as a poet and whose last poems, written while on active service, could perhaps even be deemed worthy to stand alongside those of Owen or Sassoon.

Graham Bebbington's biography ensures that Charles Masefield's brief but full life is remembered but, more than that, it offers us a window onto those fateful first years of the 20th Century. On one level it tells the story of one of many well-educated and high-minded young men whose ideals were to be put severely to the test by what they encountered in Flanders. On another level, it gives an insight into how the War affected the life of communities in North Staffordshire and sets this into the context of national events.

The author has thoroughly researched his subject and reveals for us a patriotic and conscientious individual who, in 1915, could say:

'Let us be frank with ourselves. If this war cannot cleanse us as a nation, what will?'

But who, in his last poem, has been changed by his experiences, and laments the enormity of the sacrifice that he sees around him:

'Grief though it be to die, 'tis grief yet more
To live and count the dear dead comrades o'er.'

Thanks to this book, Charles Masefield will be remembered, not just as a courageous soldier well-loved by those with whom he served, but also as a man of letters of whom his County can be proud.

Sarah Elsom DL., BA., AMA.
Trustee Staffordshire Regiment Museum

INTRODUCTION

It has been claimed that Charles John Beech Masefield MC is to Staffordshire what G. K. Chesterton and Hilaire Belloc are to Sussex. He was certainly passionate about the County as is evident from his writing. He felt that there was much in its countryside to bring *'pleasure to the eye and delight to the heart'* although largely unsung when neighbouring Counties received plaudits.

A third cousin of the Poet Laureate John Edward Masefield (1878-1967), Charles Masefield was himself a distinguished man of letters - poet, author, historian and solicitor. Unfortunately, he did not have the benefit of the length of life of his famous relative, nor that of Chesterton or Belloc. He was only 35 when he died, like thousands of other men during the Great War, paying the ultimate sacrifice in serving his country. One can only guess at what might have been his full potential.

Drawing principally on hitherto unpublished letters and other material from the Masefield family archive, this is an attempt to rediscover his story–a subject which has been neglected for far too long in my view.

1

BORN IN PUGIN LAND

Charles John Beech Masefield was born on 15th April 1882 in Cheadle, an ancient market town in the Staffordshire Moorlands approximately ten miles from the Potteries. A gateway to the richly wooded and picturesque Churnet Valley, the town nestles in the vale between the River Churnet and one of its tributaries. Cheadle is renowned for its associations with the Victorian architect Augustus Welby Pugin and the magnificent Neo-Gothic Roman Catholic Church of St. Giles, its splendidly proportioned soaring steeple of 200ft being a landmark for miles around. It is claimed to be one of the finest examples of his work. Other examples of Pugin's work in the town are the large school and priests' house and the Convent of St. Joseph. Whilst perhaps being better known for his ecclesiastical architecture, Pugin also designed a number of stations on the Churnet Valley Railway, notably Alton where he worked for John Talbot, 16th Earl of Shrewsbury, on enlargements at his residence Alton Towers. Although there are many other fine examples of Pugin's work in the County, others worthy of particular note in the immediate area include St Mary's at Uttoxeter, St John's at Cotton (under threat at the time of writing), Cotton College Chapel and the Hospital of St John at Alton. It is claimed that Pugin was 'prouder' of the latter and of Cheadle Church than any of his other buildings.[1] As a consequence, Sir Nikolaus Pevsner wrote that, *'Nowhere can one study and understand Pugin better than in Staffordshire.'* [2]

At the time of Charles Masefield's birth, Cheadle was described as being in *'a beautiful valley surrounded by lofty hills and abounding with valuable mines of coal...the town is lighted with gas, the streets paved and shops neatly fitted up.'* [3] Undoubtedly, mining was an integral part of the local economy, and Cheadle's mines were an important component of the North Staffordshire coalfield, the Park Hall Colliery being sunk in 1873. Regarded by some as 'coal town', mining was the barometer of Cheadle's fortunes. This was by no means unusual in such communities. When the mines prospered, so did the town, but when difficulties occurred such as strikes etc., the town's trade as a whole felt the impact. Annual tonnage was quoted as 21,000 in 1883, but as coal cutting became mechanised, this figure increased considerably. Equally important to the town's economy, however, was the textile industry centred on the tape and silk mills. During this period the population of Cheadle Parish was 4,492. [4] In later years, Charles Masefield himself described the town as *'standing on a hill and surrounded by other hills on almost every side. These and the abundant woods make the district one of the most attractive in Staffordshire for walking expeditions.'* [5]

Born into an old established Staffordshire family, Charles was the first child of John Richard Beech Masefield and his wife Susan. He came into the world at 'Abbots Haye', a rented property whose roots are anchored firmly in Tudor times but with Georgian and Victorian extensions to form a fine country house. At the time of Charles' birth, the Abbots Haye Estate comprised some 80 acres. Fortunately, the house exists today, being situated in Cherry Lane to the north east of the town.

The son of a respected local doctor, Charles' father was born at The Old Hall, Stone, he later being educated at Cheltenham College and Jesus College, Cambridge for which he rowed. Having graduated in law, he then became articled to Charles John Blagg of Cheadle, eventually becoming a junior partner in 1876 in the town's long established legal practice of Blagg & Son in Church Terrace. Then, in 1881, he married his employer's second daughter Susan, the couple subsequently moving to 'Rosehill' - a three storey property at Town End which he purchased from his father-in-law.

John R. B. Masefield was a keen naturalist who became a prominent member of the North Staffs. Field Club, in time holding the office of President on four occasions. Having written a number of papers on diverse subjects for the society and other organisations, he became acknowledged nationally as an eminent naturalist. A very public spirited man, he became a County Magistrate and held positions on a number of public bodies. According to the family history, John Masefield was considered to be *'a conscientious and well liked solicitor.'* [6] In similar terms, the local newspaper described him as *'possessing a bustling competence and geniality.'* ⁽⁷⁾ In later years, he worked extensively to purchase and set up the Hawksmoor Nature Reserve near Cheadle which was opened on 27th May 1922. Following his death in 1932, ornamental gates and a plaque in his memory were unveiled by his cousin, John the celebrated Poet Laureate. In its obituary column, the **Staffordshire Advertiser** described John R.B. Masefield as *'one of the best known gentlemen in the County.'* ⁽⁸⁾ The beautiful hidden gem of Hawksmoor is now in the hands of the National Trust.

Like her husband, Susan Masefield shared an interest in natural history and she supported him in his activities and research. Also keen on amateur dramatics, she regularly produced plays at the Town Hall in which friends and family participated. She served on a number of charitable association committees and further supported them by regularly organising open days and garden parties in the grounds of 'Rosehill', the family home. Susan was a good organiser, being described as *'tough'* or *'firm'* and regarded as *'a dominating character...who brought an intellectual strain'* into the Masefield family.⁽⁹⁾ Such characteristics were, no doubt, inherited from her mother, Frances, who was considered by some to be *'severe'* and *'overbearing.'* However, having had to run a large household at 'Greenhill', an extensive mansion and estate with a number of staff, and raise twelve children in the often absence of her busy husband, one can perhaps appreciate that Frances Blagg may have found herself, at times, having to exert her authority! It is understood that in the 1890s, she objected to the installation of electricity at the family home, reputedly stating that *'gas light is more flattering to my features!'* Furthermore, legend has it that at one particular coffee morning in the town, someone enquired, *'Who is that dear old lady?'* In reply, they were advised, *'That's not a dear old lady - that's Mrs Blagg!'*

Susan's father, Charles John Blagg, was also a force to be reckoned with and a moving spirit in Victorian Cheadle. Described as possessing *'true kingly power'* [10] he was always actively involved in affairs of the town, constantly at the front, and was the most redoubtable of the Blagg dynasty. In addition to being head of the busy family law practice, he was instrumental in bringing the railway to the town and the setting up of both the gas works and waterworks. A director and shareholder of many local companies, he was also a member of the Rural District Council serving as Chairman for a period. Church functions, both social and administrative, were rarely without his presence and for many years he represented the town on various bodies. Having a special interest in Church of England education, he was also concerned about the welfare of fellow townsfolk and a member of the local Board of Guardians for half a century. In 1911 he retired as Registrar of Cheadle County Court after 40 years service. As if this were not enough, he also possessed literary skills compiling, at the request of the Duke of Sutherland, *A History of the North Staffordshire Hounds and Country.* [11] In addition, he was the joint author of a biography of Bishop Richard Rawle of Trinidad, one time Rector of Cheadle.

But Charles Blagg was also a great motivator of his staff. This included the young law graduate who was to become his future son-in-law and partner in the business - John R. B. Masefield. The Masefield family would eventually join the Blaggs and other key movers and shakers of the area, playing a large part in public bodies and voluntary organisations.

Notes

1 Pevsner, *The Buildings of England – Staffordshire* (Penguin Books) p. 60.
2 *Ibid*, p. 39.
3 *Kelly's Directory 1872.*
4 Robert Plant, *History of Cheadle.*
5 Charles Masefield, *Staffordshire* (Methuen 3rd edition) pp. 109 - 110.
6 Geoffrey B. Masefield. *A History of the Senior Branch of the Masefield Family* (private publication 1975) p. 11.
7 *Cheadle & Tean Times* 6 Jan. 1933.
8 *Staffordshire Advertiser* 20 Feb. 1932.
9 Geoffrey B. Masefield, *op.cit*, p. 12.
10 *Edwardian & Great War Cheadle 1905-1918* (Cheadle & Tean Times publication 1997) p. 149.
11 Denis Stuart, *Dear Duchess* (Victor Gollancz 1982) p. 52.

John R.B. Masefield (Charles' Father)
(Photo Courtesy of Robin Masefield)

Susan Blagg (Charles' Mother)
(Photo Courtesy of Robin Masefield)

Early 20th Century Postcard of Cheadle (c.1905)
(Photo Courtesy of George Short)

Abbot's Haye, Cheadle
Birthplace of Charles Masefield in 1882
(Photo Courtesy of Mrs P. Piers-Leake)

The Wedding of Charles' Parents – John R.B. Masefield & Susan Blagg
21st June 1881
(Photo Courtesy of George Short)

2

HALCYON DAYS AT 'ROSEHILL'

In the early 20th Century, John R. B. Masefield's 'Rosehill' and Charles Blagg's Queen Anne mansion 'Greenhill' were conceived as standing *'sentinel at each end of Cheadle and seeming somehow to dominate the town.'* At this time the Blaggs and the Masefields were, apart from the rector and three doctors, the only 'gentry' in the town's population of 5,000 and consequently played a large part in local affairs and exercised great influence. In the meantime the Masefields officially achieved the status of a 'County family' in so far as is evidenced by their inclusion in **Burke's Landed Gentry** and Walford's **County Families of the United Kingdom.**[1]

'Rosehill' began life as a small 17th Century farmhouse known as 'Primrose Hill.' In 1814 it was purchased by John Blagg (grandfather of Charles J. Blagg) who renamed the property, greatly enlarged it and laid out the gardens. This remained in the hands of the

Blagg family until 1890 when it was acquired by John R. B. Masefield, from his father-in-law, having earlier married Susan Blagg. The property was then further extended, resulting in more accommodation including seven bedrooms, three bathrooms and four reception rooms, not to mention a hallway of twenty-two yards in length!

The Victorian extension work was carried out in 1893 by distinguished architect and family friend Charles Lynam (1829-1921). A founder member of the North Staffs Field Club, Lynam was a larger than life Potteries character. He built up a large private practice from his business premises in Glebe Street, Stoke-on-Trent, more or less having a total monopoly of commissions awarded by local public bodies. This resulted in contracts for such buildings as the city's public library, baths and market hall. Lynam also designed 'The Villas' - a famous cul-de-sac of twenty-four Italianate 'superior houses' off London Road, Stoke for pottery manufacturer Herbert Minton to encourage foreign artists into the area. He was also responsible for the design of a number of churches and the restoration of others in and beyond the County.

Christ Church, Fenton is considered to be his 'magnum opus.' His big passion, however, was archaeology and perhaps his greatest achievement in this respect was the unearthing of the remains of Hulton Abbey, a Cistercian house founded in 1223.

According to a former owner, 'Rosehill' was *'a lovely house with masses of character, but quite impractical for modern day living. It was built for when one could afford to have servants.'* [2] In fact, the Masefields employed four live-in domestic staff consisting of a cook, a nurse, and two housemaids. In addition, there were part-time employees such as gardeners. [3] The 'Rosehill' estate was extensive, at one time comprising 60-70 acres. Together with the house, this included stables, a walled kitchen garden, a rose garden, tennis court, woodland, and fields which were let for grazing. Seasonal produce was sold, *'being obtainable from the Masefield's gardener,'* and occasional advertisements in the **Cheadle & Tean Times** indicate that such items as *'good oak and larch stakes'* were available from the estate. Because of J. R. B Masefield's increasing interest in birds, the grounds became a virtual sanctuary with numerous nesting boxes. He also was one of the first to participate in ringing birds for observation purposes, being the author in 1897 of **Wild Bird Protection and Nesting Boxes.** In fact, records indicate that a swallow ringed on 6th May 1911 from a nest in the porch of 'Rosehill' actually flew to Natal. From this, it was discovered that swallows breeding in the British Isles migrated to winter in South Africa, something that even today we find hard to appreciate.[4] His interests also included zoology and he was the author of a number of articles in the **Victoria County History of Staffordshire.** But from a family aspect *'the glory of 'Rosehill' was the shrubberies which were particularly noted for their rhododendrons. Here devious paths wound up a steep hillside, disclosing high-level views over Cheadle and overlooked by some magnificent individual trees.*[5] This area was a virtual paradise for children and taken full advantage of by Charles who had now been joined by four siblings - Margaret Evangeline (1883); William Gordon (1885); Ethel Elizabeth Rawle (1888); and Aileen Francis Agatha (1894). A wood of some nine acres was expressly loved by the children and the scene of many picnics with hampers specially prepared by the cook. It was in this environment that they came to appreciate the birdlife, and at an early age they could recognise their songs, courtship rituals and nesting habits etc.

The Masefield children were raised in a firm, but loving environment at 'Rosehill', the household being *'a strictly Christian one.'* While there was no indulgence in drinking or smoking it was, nevertheless, regarded as *'a merry home.'* [6] John and Susan Masefield kept open house for relations and friends, arranging family parties particularly at Christmas when carol singers and hand-bell ringers would be in attendance. One particular visitor on such occasions was a young John Edward Masefield who, together with his siblings, had travelled from Herefordshire. He, in the fullness of time, would firmly establish himself as one of the best loved English poets. Throughout the years that 'Rosehill' was in the ownership of the Masefields, it was the centre of family life, deeply embedded in the affections of returning children and grandchildren as they accrued. Thus the Masefields continued to be a closely knit family.

However, apart from purely family occasions,

there were always additional activities taking place at 'Rosehill'. As a consequence of John and Susan's varied business and charitable interests, meetings, fund raising events, open days and garden parties were held on a regular basis, no doubt leaving the domestic staff little time for relaxation. For example, Susan Masefield herself was an enthusiastic committee member of a number of charitable organisations and arranged various events at the house in aid of such bodies as the Girls' Friendly Society, the Maternity Society, etc. Growing up in such an environment naturally had an influence on the Masefield children who were encouraged to participate and gradually they too, like their parents, became prominent in the society life of Cheadle.

Notes

1   Geoffrey B. Masefield, *op.cit,* pp. 30 - 31.
2   Michael Collis, Letter to author 29 Jan. 2009.
3   1901 Census.
4   Ex. information George Short.
5   Geoffrey B. Masefield, *op.cit,* p. 36.
6   *Ibid,* p. 35.

"Rosehill" Taken in 1991 showing the Victorian Extension designed by Charles Lynam
(Photo Courtesy of Michael Collis)

Distinguished Architect and Family Friend Charles Lynam
(Photo Courtesy of William Salt Library)

Young Charles Masefield
(Photo Courtesy of Robin Masefield)

3

SCHOOLDAYS

It is difficult to be precise as to when Charles Masefield's schooling actually commenced, but the family did employ a governess. Also, an area of 'Rosehill' was used, and referred to in later years, as the schoolroom. [1] One may therefore assume that his initial education and that of his siblings commenced there. Depending on her qualifications and terms of employment, the governess may possibly have received some assistance from one or more of the children's talented and capable aunts, the Blagg sisters (i.e. daughters of grand-father Charles Blagg). For example, May Adela Blagg, having been educated privately, including at a Kensington finishing school, developed into a respected astronomer and mathematician. She was eventually the first Lady Fellow of the Royal Astronomical Society. It is not generally known that the Blagg Crater on the moon is named after her. Additionally, she possessed literary skills, being the author of a children's book *Four Fairy Tales* which was published in 1911. Even so, it should also not be overlooked that the children's father's special interests included the subject of education. J. R. B. Masefield was a member of the County Education Committee, and he also served on that of the Hanley Free Library & Museum. Furthermore, he was a member of the Cheadle Committee for Science & Technical Institution. It may therefore be assumed that he would have been more than capable of employing a well qualified and/or experienced governess to ensure that his children received good tuition to provide a more than adequate introduction to meet their later educational needs.

    Nevertheless, after a while it was decided that Charles's education should be further developed by sending him to a private preparatory school at Southport. Whilst it was common practise for sons of such families to be sent away to boarding school at this time, the reasoning behind the preference for Southport and Mintholme House Preparatory School has become lost over the passage of time. It is, of course, possible that the family were familiar with the resort, having visited it. Rail travel was achievable from Staffordshire via Manchester as a result of a series of improvements and connections to the Lancashire rail network having been carried out in 1887. Southport, even then, was a popular summer and winter resort due to its *'great salubrity and the dryness of its climate'* said to be *'unequalled in England.'* [2] Whether or not Charles and his fellow pupils at Mintholme House had occasion to appreciate the resort, or had an opportunity to visit the lengthy pier with its views of the mountains of both Wales and the Lake District is not known. However, one can perhaps imagine that they may have been allowed to visit the nearby beach where the tide receded for one mile, leaving a large expanse of sand *'forming a safe and most desirable place for exercise.'* One might also assume that occasional visits were made to such venues as the aquarium at the Winter Gardens, museum, or the swimming baths, parks and botanical gardens. Perhaps the glacarium - a 'real' ice skating rink in Lord Street would also have been a popular attraction to the pupils.

Mintholme House School was one of a number of private schools in Southport in the late 19th Century. Located at 35 Park Crescent, it was administered by a Mr

Edward Clough with the assistance of members of his family. His wife Eliza was responsible for the household. His daughter Ellen occupied the post of Superintendent, with siblings Mary, Florence, Catherine and Lucy Meredith combining to form the teaching staff. The Clough's only son was the sole member of the family who was not employed in the business, working in the banking profession in the town. [3] The school appears to have gained something of an excellent reputation as an academically sound preparatory school, attracting its pupils from various parts of the country. For example, the 1891 Census reveals boarders to have originated from as far afield as London, Bournemouth and Oxford.

    A handwritten note of the period from Charles to his parents has survived in which he explains that he tried *'to get to sleep last night very hard and I counted up to one thousand and fifty!'* He also asks that, in the event of him receiving full marks for his lessons *'could we get a penny?'* Now preferring to be addressed as 'Charlie' as is evidenced from his signature, his letter is written in a beautiful clear hand, and the document is naturally precious to the family.

Mintholme House no longer exists, the site having long since been redeveloped. Furthermore, no school records appear to have survived and therefore it is uncertain what educational achievements young Charlie may have attained in his time there. However, it is evident that he had secured a good level of education by the age of 13. This is apparent by him gaining entry to the acclaimed Repton School as, at that time, the entrance examination was said to be *'tough and demanding.'* It is also perhaps worth noting that at least four members of the Blagg family had attended the Derbyshire School. This may have influenced Charlie's parents in the choice of an establishment for their son's further education.

Once the capital of the Saxon kingdom of Mercia, Repton is one of England's most ancient towns surrounded by hills and overlooking the River Trent. In the 12th Century, a great priory was founded there, but it fell into disrepair following the Dissolution of the Monasteries. On these ruins Repton School was built in 1557. Arriving at Repton in 1895, young Charlie Masefield would have probably found life at the establishment a cold water shock from that at the preparatory school. The headmaster was Dr. William Mordaunt Furneaux - otherwise 'The Boss' to pupils! According to a contemporary of Charlie's, *'there was no question that he was the headmaster both by his bearing and general conduct of affairs.'* [4] Another former pupil recalled Dr. Furneaux as *'short of stature, but of sturdy build, giving an impression of immense strength, rapid and determined in movement* (he was, in fact, a noted hurdler at Oxford) *walking generally, when alone, with a stick held horizontally in front with both hands. His features were rugged, a square resolute jaw, a quiet steady eye, and a firm mouth that could smile kindly. Though formidable, he was always approachable, an inspiring teacher, he expected from us always the best of which we were capable.'* [5]

Pupils at the school then numbered 320, and fees were £110 per annum. Boys were addressed only by their surnames and teachers wore mortar boards and gowns. Attire for pupils was straw hats throughout the year together with tail coats or Etons, but top hats were worn on Sundays for chapel services or special occasions.

As with many other public schools, Repton was

run on a 'house system' and young Charlie found himself allocated to Hall House. Each was a complete entity by itself, and its characteristics derived from those of the Housemaster and his wife. House life was based on the Study, each of which accommodated five boys or more, according to its size. A system of fagging prevailed, chiefly to keep the Study clean and tidy, and for the preparation of food. There were no prefects, the Head of Study having a recognised authority over those who were in the unit. House discipline varied according to the personality of the House Master, or in class according to that of the relevant teacher. Punishment was generally by imposition of 'lines' - the severest, according to the pupils, being 'Greek with accents'. Although Housemasters were able to 'beat a boy', those who were guilty of the more serious misdemeanours were usually referred to the Headmaster who applied the birch.

Health of pupils was catered for by the school sanatorium under the capable hands of the Matron, Miss Turner. In March 1895, there were outbreaks of measles and influenza. Several boys were 'dangerously ill' and two 14 year olds subsequently died. Surprisingly at this period, the establishment had only one bath tub, but every boy had a hot bath a week during evening prep. A cold bath was also available in the morning, but few actually made use of the facility! Dental care was administered by Mr Cave Brown of Birmingham, who attended the school regularly and as required.

Repton's curriculum was primarily Classical which was said to prepare pupils for the professions. The Modern side which catered for commerce and business was only then beginning to get into its stride in the school. However, this was the normal outlook of the Victorian age or as one pupil commented *'a boy adopted a profession - he did not merely look for a job!'* In Greek and Latin lessons there was a certain amount of 'rep' ie. learning a number of lines by heart. In later years a contemporary wrote *'in the course of five years I must have learned an enormous quantity... I never knew what virtue lay in this work...except that it was too easy for teachers.'* [6]

In the period that Charles Masefield attended Repton records indicate that the School Debating Society was extremely active. Motions covered a wide variety of topics including 'The life of a sailor is preferable to that of a soldier'; 'The introduction of conscription in England would be conducive to her safety and welfare'; 'That a tax on cycles is advisable'; 'This House is in favour of the admission of women to the Parliamentary suffrage'; 'In the opinion of this House, the glory and prosperity of England are on the decline'; 'The glory of England is due to her warriors rather than her Statesmen,' etc. As may be seen, a number of the motions debated were relevant at the time (some would contend even today!) and it would be interesting to learn if any of the debaters were eventually successful in being elected to the Palace of Westminster!

The school was also most fortunate in attracting a notable array of visiting lecturers at this time. The writer Hilaire Belloc visited on at least six occasions to talk on the subject of the French Revolution. Others included the explorer Sir Martin Conway, the missionary the Reverend J. S. Collins and a Member of the Canadian Parliament, Mr Wood.

In sport, while there was swimming with various competitions, according to contemporaries, *cricket and football were the only things that mattered.'* Success in these was *'worshipped by Masters and boys.'* Those having no aptitude for cricket were allowed bicycles which could be used for afternoon trips into the countryside. Boys who were able to skate took advantage of the exceptionally cold winter of 1895, particularly during the months of January and February. A more unusual method of keeping fit perhaps, was manning the school's fire appliance. While this was mainly used for drill purposes and involved competitions with other schools such as Rugby, it nevertheless is recorded that on one occasion it was used to extinguish a fire at a nearby cottage.

In 1897 every town, city and village in Great Britain, together with the Colonies, and dependencies of the Empire, celebrated Her Majesty Queen Victoria's Diamond Jubilee. In London on 20th June, special services were held in St. Paul's Cathedral, Westminster Abbey and St. Margaret's, Westminster attended by various members of the Royal Family and members of the House of Lords and House of Commons respectively. As for the Queen herself, now a frail 78 years old, she attended a solemn, private thanksgiving service in St. George's Chapel, Windsor. Having arrived by horse drawn carriage, she was accompanied by an Indian attendant and conveyed by wheelchair into the chapel where she remained seated throughout the ceremony. [7] However, contemporary newspaper reports of the celebrations observed that the years had left Her Majesty's intellect *'unimpaired'* and *'had given her experience in State affairs which rendered her counsel more valuable than ever.'* [8] Not to be outdone, Repton School also held its own commemorative service on the day with specially chosen hymns etc.

On the following Tuesday, 22nd June, Her Majesty was conveyed to St. Pauls with 50,000 *'picked troops'* forming part of the procession or guarding the route. The weather favoured the day and enthusiastic crowds greeted the Queen on her journey to the cathedral. At Repton, boys who could arrange to attend the procession and celebrations in London with their parents were allowed to do so, departing by special train. Those who remained at the school 'escaped' lessons and were entertained with a cricket match and fireworks in the evening.

Pupils were also able to take advantage of applying for special leave to attend the Jubilee Naval Review at Spithead with their parents. The press reported that *'no such spectacle of strength and splendour was ever seen before…a proof of England's command of the sea.'* In addition to the Royal Naval shipping, international vessels also attended the event representing Germany, Turkey, Holland, Norway, Russia, Spain, France, Portugal and America. Vast crowds watched the spectacle on both sides of the Solent. [9] Those Repton pupils who were unable to attend the event remained in school, but were given a days' holiday. Whether Charles Masefield attended the celebrations in London or at Portsmouth is not known, but it would not be surprising if he did so in the company of his parents.

As in many schools, Repton had a number of societies including photographic, natural sciences etc. To encourage further interest, some offered prizes annually for associated themes or topics, including awards for such initiatives as the best collection of botany, and another for butterflies. It is believed that young Charlie would have participated in such activities, having seemingly inherited a genetic thread to his father's interests and association with the North Staffs Field Club. In any event, his parents openly encouraged their children to take an interest in natural history and the countryside.

Repton's magnificent archives also reveal that in 1898 Charlie was successful in gaining the Aylmer Prize for Divinity. Donated in memory of Charles Paget Aylmer, a pupil who died at the school in 1890, the award was for the best paper submitted on a theological subject. Further distinction followed in 1899, his final year, when he succeeded in winning the Howe Prize for English Verse with his composition '*A Vision of Italian Painters.*' Although some prize winning works were published in the school's magazine **Rectangle,** sadly those of Charles Masefield do not appear to feature. However, one can imagine that winning both the Aylmer and Howe prizes was evidence of the emergence of his literary skills, possibly resulting from the encouragement of a particular teacher and, of course, his parents. Although poetry was not a strong subject at Repton at this time pupils were, nevertheless, studying Tennyson and the other Victorian poets.

In the meantime, the decision had been taken that on leaving the school, young Charlie would follow his father into the legal profession.

Notes

1   1901 Census & information from Michael Collis.
2   *Slater's Directory 1890.*
3   *Ibid,* 1892.
4   A. L Hadow, Memoir in Repton Archives.
5   R. F. Peachey, Memoir in Repton Archives.
6   A. L. Hadow, *op.cit.*
7   *Staffordshire Sentinel* 21 June 1897.
8   *Ibid,* 22 June 1897.
9   *Ibid,* 28 June 1897.

The Municipal Gardens Southport
Early 20th Century Postcard of Southport (from Author's Collection)

Shopping Promenade, Southport
Early 20th Century Postcard of Southport (from Author's Collection)

The Promenade, Southport
Early 20th Century Postcard of Southport (from Author's Collection)

Dr William Mordaunt Furneaux, Headmaster of Repton School
(Photo Courtesy of Repton School)

Repton School photographed in the Early 1890s
(Photo Courtesy of Repton School)

4

THE LEGAL PROFESSION & LITERARY CONNECTIONS

In 1899 Charles Masefield found himself in a position of employment not unlike that of Uriah Heep, the slimy articled clerk in Charles Dickens classic ***David Copperfield.*** Even so, being articled to his father, Charles would not have been, to use Dickens terms, expected to *'aspire to be umble'* (sic) like Heep, but completely the opposite.

Having joined the busy practice of Blagg, Son & Masefield, he entered the 'mysterious' world (to outsiders!) of solicitors and the legal profession at their offices at Church Terrace, abutting Cheadle's Anglican Church of St. Giles the Abbot. At that time, the firm was dominated by the Blagg family who were, in effect, his relations! The head of the practice was the indomitable Charles John Blagg who was always addressed as 'Sir' by the staff. In addition to Charles's father, the firm's other solicitors were two uncles - Walter Edward Blagg, a veteran of the Boer War, and Ernest William Halcombe

Blagg.

The practice acted for all the area's major landowners and industrialists including the colliery owners and ironstone masters. According to Michael Collis, whose father subsequently purchased the practice in 1945, they *'took on any matter which their clients required.'* For example, they collected rents for landowners on quarter days, hiring Longton Town Hall for that purpose. Also, being agents for the Royal Exchange for a lengthy period, they collected premiums. However, their main area of work was conveyancing and probate for the landowning classes, also undertaking litigation as required. In this respect, records survive indicating that in 1876 they hired rooms for a period of five days at the Swan Hotel, Stafford to provide facilities for a case at the Assizes. The practice was also involved in such enterprises as the building of the Cheadle railway, and they circulated brochures canvassing subscribers. Charles Blagg himself took the chair at public meetings concerning the matter, also travelling to London to represent his clients' interests at the Parliamentary Committee. [1] Indeed, Charles Blagg constantly appeared in the news, his speeches on various topics being recorded in both the local and national newspapers. Yet for all his attributes, he appeared unable (or unwilling!) to accept 'modern technology' in the office! For example, the law practice acquired the second of the town's telephone installations, but the head of the firm would not use it! As a consequence, his secretary and other members of staff constantly had to relay messages to him. Legend has it that he would declare *'I will not use that infernal machine - tell him to write!'* [2]

Having by this time had some experience of law and life in the practice, Charles wrote an article in 1903 entitled '***A day of my life***' for the monthly magazine ***The Treasury***. Using a pseudonym, as solicitors were not permitted to advertise, he described a typical day in his work schedule. *'Having cycled to work,'* he wrote, *'I then 'plunged' at once into the task of dealing with the morning's correspondence. Of these, about half of the letters were capable of being answered with replies dictated to a shorthand clerk.'* This is interesting in itself, as Blaggs did have some typewriters by the late 1890s but Charles's clerk, it appears, would have written replies by hand. After this, Charles describes various callers including *'a clerk from a neighbouring solicitors to settle a purchase of land, an irate Parish Councillor and a visit from an important 17 stone prosperous, good humoured landowner who caused the narrow stairs to creak announcing his arrival!'* The article then describes his attendance on 'court day' as magistrate's clerk for the morning session and of the trying of offending *'drunks'*, a case of *'furious driving'* and a couple involving *'unlicensed dogs'*. After lunch in a local *'eating house'* he writes that he received an urgent request to attend a farmer to prepare *'a death bed will.'* This was then drafted and formally executed by the dying man and attested by the Parish Priest. Charles then concludes that he succeeded in *'winning another race against the Great Destroyer!'*

The magazine article also describes the room in which he worked at the offices. He wrote that he could not pretend that it was *'greatly distinguished for the beauty of appearance or richness of furniture,'* but for him *'it was not without a certain charm - the charm which hangs about all things which form a part of one's daily life.*

Beyond three chairs, a desk and an almanac or two, it contains nothing but papers - papers in boxes, papers in cupboards, papers tied with red tape in bundles on my desk.' [3] The article provides a fascinating insight into life in a lawyer's office in a North Staffordshire market town at the turn of the 20th Century. By coincidence, Michael Collis occupied that same room on joining the practice in 1952 as an articled clerk. He found that little had changed from Charles's description. In fact, some of the original files going back to the 1890s remained in the cupboards *'providing a wonderful time warp.'* [4]

Having had his prose sketch of a day in a solicitor's life published, Charles was also drawn to verse. Fortunately, a number of these early efforts have survived, although they were not published in his lifetime. An early example is the poem ***Dawn*** composed in April 1901. Said to provide evidence of his *'sensitive spirit'* and *'deep susceptibility to natural beauty'* the opening lines are:-

'The breeze thro' the pine branches softly is sighing'
Fast home to the darkness the owlets are flying,
The woods are awaking, for night lies a-dying,

And Dawn cometh fast.'

Another sample of his work from the period is the poem **Bell Rhymes:-**
'This metal with fire was tempered well
Ere men could make it a perfect bell;
When thou through the fire has passéd too,
God grant thy soul may ring as true.

Twixt heaven and earth I hang and share
In God's own thoughts - then, waking, tell
The message that I gather there
To all whose ears are tunéd well'. [5]

On eventually being admitted a solicitor in 1905, Charles Masefield practised for a short period in Derby, later joining Shelton & Co., whose practice was at 47 Queen Street, Wolverhampton. In 1908 he was taken into partnership which led to him being placed in charge of the office. [6] At this time, he was residing at 141 Tettenhall Road in the town.

While living and working in the so-called 'Capital

of the Black Country', Charles was surprisingly most active on the literary front, given that he was now fully responsible for the busy local law practice. Continuing to pursue his interests, he joined the area Literary Club which met at the Star & Garter Hotel, serving as Honorary Secretary for a period. Here, he was in distinguished company as its President was none other than the writer Hilaire Belloc. Furthermore, others who had occupied the office previously included Jerome K. Jerome, G. K. Chesterton and Sir Herbert Beerholm Tree. Charles's first serious essay in authorship followed in 1908 with the publication of the novel ***Gilbert Hermer***. Published by Blackwood, the plot is set in the immediate neighbourhood of Cheadle which he called 'Cradleby'. The local 18th Century Hales Hall is thinly disguised as Adams Hall and the hero resided in one of the characteristic old tollgate houses. The local press described the work as *'a most attractive and readable novel.'* [7]

In the meantime, Charles's attention had been drawn to the gentler sex, he having met and fallen in love with a former school friend of his sister Elizabeth (Betty).

Muriel Agnes Bussell was the youngest daughter of the late Rev'd F. Vernon Bussell MA., one time Vicar of Balderton, and Mrs M. Bussell. Evidence of their advanced wedding plans survives in the form of a letter written by Charles to Muriel whilst travelling on a train. In this he assures her that the *'whole of the feminine portion at home seems quite thoroughly pleased with the bridesmaid frock design'* etc. He concludes by adding *'this letter has been sadly business-like, but you can read love between the lines.'* [8]

The marriage ceremony took place on 9th June 1910 in the magnificent setting of the ancient Priory Church in Great Malvern. A lengthy report in the local newspaper reveals that the *'fully choral'* service was conducted by the Rev'd F. W. Bussell DD., Vice Principal of Brasenose College, Oxford (cousin of the bride) assisted by Rev'd W. B. Masefield (cousin of the bridegroom). In reporting details of the wedding ensembles, the journalist makes special mention of brooches worn by the four bridesmaids consisting of Stafford knots in pearl and turquoises - the gifts of the bridegroom. At the close of the service the organist played Mendelssohn's 'Wedding March' and the church bells rang out their joyous proclamation that the ceremony was complete. Guests then returned to the reception which was held at the home of the bride's mother in nearby Wyche Road. As was customary during this period in reporting such items of news, full details were listed of the 140 or so wedding presents. This included a gold watch chain and a bicycle which were exchanged between the newly wedded couple. Later in the day, Charles and Muriel left for their honeymoon in Southern Ireland. [9]

During their absence, Charles's *Staffordshire* was published in Methuen's series of 'Little Guides on English Counties'. To obtain material for this, he is reputed to have meticulously visited every Parish in the County but one, travelling by train and bicycle. According to his friend Dr. Charles Henry Poole, the work was *'a labour of love'* for *'he loved every inch of the County of his birth.'* [10] Now a collectors' item, this fascinating compilation is dedicated to *'all those who are, to the dead who have been, and to the unborn who will be lovers of Staffordshire.'* Although only of pocket size, the illustrated work covers history, archaeology, scenery, climate, communications, industries and the flora and fauna of the County. In his preface, the author dismisses those who regard Staffordshire as *'something of a slut among the Counties'* rightly contending that *'much of its scenery is beautiful.'* The volume was subsequently described as *'the best guide to Staffordshire.'* [11]

Meanwhile, it may not have gone unnoticed by the family that Charles's third cousin John Edward Masefield had begun to write seriously and was attracting attention with the publication of his **Salt Water Ballads** (1902), **Ballads** (1903), and **Ballads & Poems** *(1910).* Some of the poems contained in the works such as **Sea Fever** and **Cargoes** have remained popular, providing the first introduction to poetry for generations of schoolchildren. Coincidentally, the future Poet Laureate's work had also attracted the attention of Millicent, Duchess of Sutherland. She was in the process of compiling an anthology of contemporary poetry and used her influence and contacts to enlist the services of eminent poets of the day. Published in 1904 by Constable under the title of **The Wayfarer's Love,** all profits from the volume went to

Millicent's favourite charity, the Potteries & Newcastle Cripples' Guild. Contributors included G. K. Chesterton, W. B. Yeats, A. E. Housman, etc. and John Masefield's poem *Being her Friend* was featured in the collection.

In 1911 Charles and Muriel Masefield celebrated the birth of a son, Geoffrey Bussell Masefield. He was born on 16th June at the home of his parents, 141 Tettenhall Road, Wolverhampton. His naming broke a long tradition in the Masefield family whereby the eldest son should have either William or John as one of his Christian names. That same year saw publication of the first collection of Charles's poems. Published by A. C. Fifield of London, the volume was entitled *The Season's Differences and Other Poems*. According to the journalist, novelist and poet Arthur St. John Adcock (1864-1930), in this collection of works '*you make contact with a mind that is keenly susceptible to natural beauty and to what is finest in the nature of man.*'$^{(12)}$ On learning of the publication, the local *Cheadle & Tean Times* appeared to be surprised that Charles had now turned his interest to verse from prose - '*his mental activities are astonishing although it is only what we may expect from a son of clever progenitors on both sides.'* The newspaper *'heartily wished the work the greatest success'* and then featured a number of reviews from other journals. For example, the **Times Literary Supplement** found that the volume *'suggests reflections revealing a personality whose thought expresses itself in well-chiselled verse throughout the interesting little collection.'* On the other hand, the **Staffordshire Advertiser** concluded that *'the author is an accomplished writer of graceful verse, and the poems which the book contains are pitched in various keys. 'Loves Riches' is a tuneful rhapsody on the old theme ever new. 'Enslaved' is the subject of a well-twinned sonnet, and one of the prettiest poems in the book is entitled 'Morning in June'.* Similarly, the **Sheffield Daily Telegraph** found the poem **'Song: if in thy heart'** *'delightful'* and **'Gwaelod: The Submerged Kingdom'** to be *'well done'*. In addition, the reviewer concluded that the little volume was worth purchasing for **'The Besieged Captain to his men'**. The **Manchester Guardian** reviewer declared that *'the name of Masefield is closely associated in our minds with poetic achievement and fresh possibilities of poetry. Charles*

*Masefield's volume will not tend to weaken the association...His workmanship is always clean and often beautiful. The short lyric '**The Fault**' is perhaps the most perfect of his compositions.'* [13]

Following the earlier success of his pocket guide **Staffordshire**, Charles approached the publisher Macmillan with a proposal that he might write a work on 'Highways & Byways of Staffordshire'. Their famous series of works on the counties had first appeared in 1897 and 21 titles were in print when Charles's **Staffordshire** was published. However, Macmillan were unwilling at that time to pursue the suggestion contending that '*the series was not a sufficiently paying venture even for more attractive counties!*' [14] It appears that Macmillan did have a policy of only considering publishing volumes on those counties that '*would be of more interest*'. Nevertheless, the company did confirm that what success they did have with the series was probably due to the illustrations and careful choice of counties. [15]

Notes

1. Michael Collis, Letter to author, 15 May 2009
2. Michael Collis, Letter to author, 17 Aug 2009
3. *The Treasury* Sep 1903.
4. Michael Collis, *op.cit.*
5. Charles J. B. Masefield, *Poems* (Blackwell) 1919.
6. Company Circular, March 1908.
7. *Cheadle & Tean Times,* 8 Dec 1911.
8. Letter dated 7 March 1910.
9. *Malvern Gazette,* 10 June 1910.
10. *Poets of the Shires – Staffordshire,* (N. Ling & Co 1925) p. 275.
11. *Cheadle & Tean Times.* 8 Dec 1911.
12. *For Remembrance - soldier poets who have fallen in the war* (Hodder & Stoughton) p. 130.
13. *Cheadle & Tean Times, op.cit.*
14. 'In Memoriam' in *Trans. North Staffs Field Club,* Vol. L11 1917-18, p. 108.
15. Macmillan, Letter to author, 13 Dec 2010.

Plaque of Blagg, Son & Masefield Solicitor's Office premises
(Photo Courtesy of Michael Collis)

Newspaper Photo of the Wedding of Charles & Muriel Masefield
(Photo Courtesy of Robin Masefield)

Charles Masefield with baby Geoffrey (1911)
(Photo Courtesy of Robin Masefield)

Marriage Certificate of Charles & Muriel Masefield
(Photo Courtesy of Robin Masefield)

Former Offices of Blagg, Son & Masefield, Church Terrace, Cheadle
(Photographed by Lynne M. Bebbington, 2009)

Looking East along Cheadle High Street (c. 1909)
(Photo Courtesy of George Short)

The West End of Cheadle High Street (c. 1903)
(Photo Courtesy of George Short)

5

RETURN TO CHEADLE

In 1912 Charles Masefield returned to the employment of Blagg, Son & Masefield at Cheadle upon the retirement of his father. The practice continued to be under the control of the indefatigable Charles Blagg, now in his 80th year, and showing no indication of retiring. Even at that age, he is said to have had '*a fine presence*' and, having a long white beard, '*was the embodiment of an Old Testament patriarch.*' At a family wedding he is reputed to have expressed amusement that his son-in-law (i.e. John - Charles' father) '*some 20 years his junior, should give up the cares of business, leaving him at 80 to continue!*' [1]

On their return to Cheadle, the choice of residence for Charles and Muriel Masefield and baby son Geoffrey was 'Hanger Hill' at Town End which abutted 'Rosehill', his parent's home.

A wicket gate connected the two properties enabling access without actually having to make use of the highway. According to the family, the domestic establishment at 'Hanger Hill' was *'modest'*. Nevertheless, the staff comprised 3 maids, a nanny and part-time gardener. [2]

Already a member of the North Staffs Field Club, Charles became more active in its affairs on his return, eventually becoming Vice-President. His father was, by this time, a very prominent member having himself served four terms as President. Records indicate that Charles led excursions, also serving as a member of the NSFC's Publication & Wall Excavation Committees and of the Archaeology Section. Largely, through his initiative, a fund was raised by subscription among members for restoration of 14th Century brasses in churches at Audley, Clifton Campville and Norbury. Like his father, Charles was a very public spirited person with wide interests in life.

In the early 20th Century, there were many opportunities in Cheadle for those who wished to gain benefit from further education and/or to improve their understanding of current affairs. Among these was the North Staffordshire Miners' Higher Education Movement. Founded in 1910 by Charles Masefield, the

Branch ran a series of lectures on various topics including Russia, and 'The making of the German Empire' etc. Charles was also *one of the prominent Church people of Cheadle'* who staged plays to raise funds for the Parish Church. The productions ranged from farce to Shakespeare. Together with Charles, 'stalwarts' of the drama group included his brother and sisters. Calling themselves the 'Twelve Midsummer Crickets', they attracted good sized audiences, the last mention appearing to be in July 1914. It was then that they staged the comedy 'David Garrack' at the Town Hall in aid of the Church Schools' Building Fund. [3] It may be said that variety entertainment and concerts played a large part in the social life of the town at this time.

But it was also a period when most families were without any means of private transport. Cheadle was no exception but there were, at times, opportunities to travel further afield by means of organised excursions. Charles and his father are known to have assisted in arranging trips using hired brakes to tour the local countryside in conjunction with nature study courses. The bicycle was also a popular means of transport for some. These could be purchased from a number of establishments in the town which also provided a repairs service. Bicycles could also be hired from the Royal Oak Hotel where cyclists met regularly. Even the local Rambling Club had a cycling section! A keen cyclist himself, Charles used his machine as a means of transport for business. Also, having presented his wife with a bicycle on the occasion of their wedding, he introduced her to the delights of the local countryside. Then, as their son grew older, the couple took him with them into the surrounding area in order that he too could appreciate its attractiveness. To this day, many hold the view that the valley of the River Churnet has some of the loveliest countryside in England.

In the midst of all his activities, Charles continued to compose poetry, but also for the first time experimented with the writing of a drama. Entitled **Quite Impossible**, a draft was submitted to Wyndham's Theatre, London. In reply, the actor/manager Gerald du Maurier wrote that he considered *'the characterisation and dialogue to be very good'* but it was *'not the kind of play that would be suitable for this theatre.'* [4] Sadly, no further details of the play are known, as the script does not appear to have survived. On the other hand, in 1914 Charles enjoyed additional success with the publication of a further selection of his poems under the title ***Dislikes - some modern satires***. Again published by A. C. Fifield of London, Arthur St. John Adcock described the work as *'not satire that burns in the last poem in the book -* ***Beauty Cast Out*** *- but a passionate earnestness of regret that the England of those latter years should, in Jonson's phrase, 'let the noble and the precious go' in the wealth and material prosperity, that in her great towns the sense of beauty and the desire of it should have been banished by the lust for power and commercial gain.'*

The following is an extract from the poem referred to -

O pagan towns!
O Birmingham, idolatrous and blind!
O Liverpool, where aspiration drowns
Beneath the surges and the chilling wind
Of the sea commerce, can your riches clothe your shame?
O Manchester and Glasgow and Belfast,
To unborn epochs what of noble fame
Bequeath you when your prospering hour has passed?'

In a lighter vein, evidence of Charles Masefield's sense of humour is also featured in the book, in particular the poem ***A Musical Comedy Alphabet*** –
'A's the lascivious Author who wrote It;
B are the Britons who 'toppin stuff' vote It;
C is the Censor, whose taste It just fits;
D is the Dubious state of his wits…'

Another wonderful example is ***The Honours List*** in which a child asks her father what *'that glorious list'* is all about, and his answers remain relevant today!
'Can you tell me, dear Pater, his daughter inquired,
The reason of what seems so queer
In the list that the papers all print in large type
On this, the first day of the year?....'

During this period, the population in Britain was rising and there was much unemployment. Regardless of this, life for the Masefield family in general appeared comfortable. Also, having returned to Cheadle and living in close proximity, Charles was able to see more of his parents and unmarried sisters who remained at home. They were a closely knit family and participated in such regular events as the ritual family tea party at 'Rosehill' every Sunday. On such occasions, proud grandparents, including C. J. Blagg, were able to share the company of, and become more acquainted with Charles and Muriel's young son Geoffrey. 'Rosehill' was truly the centre of family activities, another regular guest being Aubrey Bowers. A cousin of Charles, Aubrey was the owner of Caverswall Castle, a Jacobean manor house situated a short distance from the town. Visits here were regarded as very popular by the Masefields who would often be collected by dog-cart which would be specially dispatched from Caverswall for them. The historic property was a marvellous place for young Geoffrey to play, often playing hide and seek in the seemingly endless rooms and corridors with Aubrey's daughter Penelope, just as Charles and his siblings had done years before. If they happened to get lost in the building, they were usually 'rescued' by Miss Gibson, Penelope's governess, who was very popular with the children.

But this seemingly idyllic atmosphere was soon to be changed by events in Europe and which would eventually have implications not only for the Masefields, but for the majority of families in Britain. In 1914, the nations of Europe were divided into two major power blocks - Germany & Austria-Hungary; and France, Russia & Great Britain. However, the stability of the Austro-Hungarian Empire was being threatened by the rise of Slav nationalism in its southern provinces.

The Austrian government viewed Serbia as the instigator of the Slav demands for independence. The situation worsened when on 28th June, during a state visit to the Serbian capital of Sarajevo, the heir to the Austrian throne, Archduke Franz Ferdinand, was assassinated by a Serbian nationalist. As a consequence, Austria made a series of demands on the Serbian government and when these were not complied with, war was declared on 28th July. On the following day, Austria began the bombardment of Belgrade which resulted in Russia mobilising her army in support of the beleaguered Serbs. This, in turn, lead to full German mobilisation in support of Austria. On 2nd August, Germany sent an ultimatum to the Belgian government demanding free passage for her troops. Germany had, in effect, declared war on France following an alleged incident involving the bombing by a

French aviator of a railway line near Karlsruhe and Nuremburg. In the meantime, Belgium had refused to allow its neutrality to be violated but nevertheless on 4th August German troops entered the country. Therefore, at this time, a European war had commenced with Austria-Hungary & Germany on the one hand, and Serbia, Russia & France on the other. In the beginning Britain remained non-committal, not supporting one side or the other. Many were of the opinion that it was not their concern if the nations of Europe went to war, whilst also, perhaps, hoping that war would be averted. Even so, when the Germans violated Belgian neutrality, Britain issued an ultimatum demanding that all German forces be withdrawn from the country. In effect, Britain was bound by a treaty of alliance signed in 1839. When a withdrawal was not forthcoming, at the height of a long hot summer, Britain, on 4th August, declared war on Germany.

It was the end of an era. The stately pace of life was to change completely. But could Charles Masefield perhaps have had a premonition when in October 1911 he wrote the lines -

'The morning burns; and I my sword must take,

And all my arms, as my fathers did....?
(from **The Unknown***).*

Notes

1   F. J. Johnson (ed) *Edwardian & Great War Cheadle* (Cheadle & Tean Times) p. 150.
2   Geoffrey B. Masefield, *op.cit,* p. 31.
3   F. J. Johnson, *op.cit,* p. 99.
4   Letter dated 16 June 1914.

Family Group Photo (Left – Right) C.J. Blagg, Muriel Masefield, Charles Masefield, Susan Masefield & Young Geoffrey in front (1913)
(Photo Courtesy of Robin Masefield)

Hanger Hill, Cheadle
(Photographed by Lynne M. Bebbington, 2009)

C. J. Blagg – 'The Grand Old Man of Cheadle'
(Photo Courtesy of George Short)

6

WAR-OPENING MOVES

Britain's first blow in the war was struck by the Royal Navy when, on 5th August 1914, the German minesweeper Konigin Luise was sunk while on duty in the North Sea. [1] On mainland Europe, events also moved ahead apace with Austria-Hungary invading Serbia on 12th August. In turn, German troops in their occupation of Belgium burned the city of Louvain. Then, on 16th August Liege fell, the Germans making use of their heavy railway guns including the infamous 'Big Bertha'. Although Belgian forces resisted fiercely, they were pushed back across the country but in the meantime the British Expeditionary Force (BEF) had arrived, reaching Mons on 20th August. Two days later, the first encounter between British and German troops took place. The British held their positions but, with the withdrawal of French troops, the situation became intolerable and eventually they were forced to retreat to the north east of Paris. The Battle of Mons resulted in around 1500 British casualties and 5000 for the Germans and held up their advance, giving the Allies valuable breathing space. The action resulted in the German Kaiser ridiculing the British force as *'a contemptible little army'*, a remark he would, in time, come to regret. As for the British, they dubbed themselves 'the Old Contemptibles'.

There then followed a period in which both sides attempted to outflank each other. In the race, the Allies moved leftwards whilst the Germans advanced to the right, each hoping to move into open countryside against the rear of the enemy. What stopped the moves was the sea, and from here both sides had little choice but to dig in. This resulted in the birth of the defensive front line trench system, which eventually stretched from the North Sea at Nieuport in Belgium to the French Alps with opposing armies facing each other. In general, each side's trenches were interconnected and could be 6-10ft deep, revetted and sandbagged and dug in zig-zag formation to limit the impact of explosives. The area between opposing trenches then became known as 'No Man's Land' and this, in places, was only 50yds in width. In the course of events, the BEF moved to Flanders in September whereupon, being closer to the Channel ports, its supply lines with England were shortened.

In the meantime, a rather unexpected person happened to arrive in the war zone. By coincidence, Millicent, Duchess of Sutherland, and a friend of Charles J. Blagg, had left for France on 8th August and was one of the first British women to organise a hospital unit. The war proved to be a liberation for many women, whether titled or not. They saw it as an opportunity to exploit unexpected talents and personal aspirations. Some became nurses or nursing probationers in support of the war effort, while others took on certain roles of those men who had enlisted. Millicent's unit was initially in France and subsequently transferred to Belgium where, unfortunately, she and her medical team were caught up in the initial hostilities at Namur when it fell to German troops. Even so, she and her nurses continued to tend the wounded of both sides before eventually being granted authority to leave occupied territory. To raise funding to allow her to return to France with an ambulance unit, the Duchess then wrote an account of her experiences. Under the title ***Six Weeks at the War***, this was published by ***The Times*** newspaper. In later years, Millicent was awarded the Belgian Royal Red Cross and the French Croix de Guerre for her services. [2]

Soon after hostilities commenced, reports of atrocities began to be received which outraged public opinion across the world. For example, when Antwerp was captured by the Germans, the clergy were ordered to ring the church bells but declined to do so. Subsequently, the French journal **Le Matin** reported that *'the barbaric conquerors of Antwerp punished the unfortunate Belgian priests for their heroic refusal to ring the church bells by hanging them as living clappers to the bells with their heads down.'* [3]

On 7th August, Secretary of State for War Lord Kitchener issued an appeal for 100,000 men to join the British army. As a result, a patriotic enthusiasm swept through the country with huge crowds gathering outside recruiting offices, no doubt spurned on by Kitchener's now famous 'Your Country Needs You' iconic mobilisation campaign posters, and driven on by thoughts of idealism, adventure and foreign travel. On the other hand it must be said that for those living in extreme poverty, the war offered clothes, shelter and food.

Within a month of war being declared, Cheadle witnessed the first departure of those who had responded to the call to arms. In reporting the event, ***The Cheadle & Tean Times*** noted that 76 men left midst *'stirring scenes'*. Accompanied by the Cheadle Subscription Band, they marched to the railway station where they were provided with a meal and cigarettes before boarding the train. [4]

Also at the outbreak of the conflict, a horse requisition scheme was implemented to produce sufficient animals to support the BEF. In the past these had been drawn from businesses with large horse fleets such as bus and tram companies, breweries, etc. These animals were usually healthy, strong and ideal for pulling the guns and heavy equipment. However, by this period, due to mechanisation of transport, the number of horse drawn passenger vehicles had reduced, resulting in this form of supply being severely diminished. Nonetheless, the War Department embarked on its requisitioning scheme and in the month of August 140,000 were impressed in 12 days, mainly farm and van horses. Fortunately, Kitchener had foreseen that this figure could be woefully inadequate, and a specialist team had already been despatched to the United States and Canada to purchase additional animals. By 1918, 1 million had been purchased and shipped from these sources.

On 7th August, Cheadle itself participated in the requisitioning scheme. Horses were taken to the Wheatsheaf Hotel yard where they were examined by local veterinary surgeon John Edward Hutchinson MRCVS, and a colleague. Those animals chosen were then branded and reassembled on the following Monday in the Market Square from whence they left the town under the charge of the army. [5]

In addition to the farming community, a number of businesses in North Staffordshire supplied horses for the war effort. These included the Silverdale Co-operative Society and breweries. Even so, while the requisitioning was generally accepted as an essential part of the mobilisation, it was perhaps inevitable that complaints would be received from the farming community on the ground that loss of animals would have a detrimental effect on the harvesting of crops, etc. After all, feeding of the population was a necessity whether in wartime or not.

Purchasing of horses was the responsibility of the

Army Remount Service, a department of the War Office. Its depots received newly purchased animals and held them until they were seen to be fit for issue to a unit. Most would have been broken in before purchase. Any further schooling which may have been required, say for ceremonial or tactical work, was usually undertaken after joining the respective regiments.

The nearest Remount Depot to Cheadle was located at Trentham Hall Stables. Part of Northern Command, records indicate that it was a very well run establishment which could handle '*500-1500 horses at a time, or even more!*' Here, '*farsighted business methods*' were used in running the unit, and '*every penny of profit*' *expended on improving facilities.* ' [6] The Trentham Depot was also served by a branch at Butterton Hall, some 4 miles distant. Staff stationed there happened to regard the location as '*a fearfully backwoods place to be stuck in - no excitement whatever, apart from remount work.*' To spend an evening in Hanley, staff had to drive the 3 miles in a dog cart into Newcastle-under-Lyme and then take a tram.[7] Coincidentally, in 1914/15 Butterton Hall was the headquarters of the $2^{nd}/5^{th}$ North Staffordshire

Regiment.[8]

Meanwhile, harrowing stories of German use of brute force and treatment of local people continued to feature in the newspapers, fuelling the patriotic enthusiasm sweeping the country. On 4th September 1914 *The Cheadle & Tean Times* published an extract from *The Sunday Chronicle* warning of 50,000 aliens (i.e. non-British) who were free to carry on their businesses and enjoy the privilege of British citizenship. In Cheadle itself, rumours were rife relating to local pharmacist Frederic Hanna whose premises were in Cross Street. This resulted in Blagg, Son & Masefield inserting a public notice in the local newspaper threatening to take legal proceedings against anyone spreading *'wild and slanderous rumours that he was a German subject, or foreigner, under police supervision.'* In any event, it transpired that the allegations were without foundation as Mr Hanna was, in fact, born in Ashton-under-Lyne of Scottish parents! [9]

As the year was drawing to a close, it became clear that the war would *not* be over by Christmas. This was emphasised even more when hostilities were brought closer to home with the bombardment of Scarborough on 16th December by two German battle cruisers. Later they turned their attention to Whitby and Hartlepool. Altogether, 122 people were killed and 443 injured, with much damage to property.

On the Western Front it rained relentlessly during the months of November and December. Founded on clay, drainage from the flat and fertile fields of Flanders tends to be slow. Describing the soils during such wet periods as *'heavy going'* can be an understatement as troops of both sides could testify. Trenches were progressively formed into quagmires, being flooded to a depth of 2ft or more in places and, at times, military operations were brought to a standstill. Horses were drowned in the ensuing mud, as were hundreds of field mice and frogs which had fallen into the trenches and were unable to escape. According to military historian Martin J. Farrar, the BEF in 1914 was *'incomparably the best trained, best organised and best equipped British Army which ever went forth to war.'* However, where it fell short of the enemy was *'first and foremost in numbers.'* Also, for trench warfare, it was *'almost wholly deficient.'* [10] In any event, all the gadgets and weapons that we associate today with trench warfare were, at the time, still on the drawing board, or being tested for the first time. These included hand grenades, trench mortars, and even 'duckboards' for the floors of the trenches. [11]

Apart from wounds and the accidents of war, 'trench foot' was quite a common complaint among the troops. This was caused by wearing wet boots in the dreadful conditions of the trenches, and being unable to dry them properly between periods of action. Sanitary arrangements were also rudimentary and the effects from infectious diseases were exacerbated by the sheer numbers of men living in close proximity. Frostbite was also common in winter and boils were endemic as a result of duty clothing chafing the skin. Rats were also a constant problem in the trenches. When anything was missing, rats were often the cause, just as they were responsible for equipment and packs being torn, or emergency rations lost. However, on rare occasions, owls would provide a temporary solution. Some survivors of the war recalled the spectacle of a barn owl descending on silent wings to snatch up a victim. The rats would scurry for cover, but then return when they deemed it safe a few minutes later.

By complete contrast, weather conditions had improved by 24th December and were described as being *'perfect for a Christmas card.'* Frost had transformed the landscape with the mud hardened and pools frozen. The Western Front quietened down to the extent that in some sectors there was a brief interlude in hostilities. Famously, enemy shook hands with enemy in No Man's Land, sang to each other and exchanged souvenirs, some even playing football. This peaceable period, which was witnessed by men of the 1st Battalion, North Staffordshire Regiment, was also seen as a suitable time for the decent burial of the dead, the bodies of whom had been lying in No Man's Land for weeks. [13]

However, both sides also took the opportunity to build or rebuild front line and communication trenches and dug-outs ready for a Spring offensive. While Kitchener's mobilisation campaign had achieved excellent results by the end of 1914 in attracting over one million recruits, it became clear that more troops would definitely be needed.

Notes

1 Malcolm Thomson, *Churchill–His Life and Times* (Odhams Press, 1965) p. 151.
2 Denis Stuart, *op.cit*, pp. 125-8.
3 Robert Graves, *Goodbye to All That* (Penguin Books, 1960) p. 69.
4 F. J. Johnson, *op.cit*, p. 172.
5 *Ibid*, p. 172.
6 Public Record Office Ref WO107/26.
7 Correspondence of Mrs M. Overton. 6 Feb 1918. (Author's collection)
8 Lt. Walter Meakin, *The 5th North Staffords & the North Midland Territorials 1914-18*. (Longton: Hughes & Harber, 1920) pp. 12, 71.
9 F. J. Johnson, *op.cit*, p. 171.
10 *News from the Front* (Sutton Publishing, 1998) p. 34.
11 *Ibid*, p. 42.
12 Robert Graves, *op.cit*, p. 180.
13 Malcolm Brown & Shirley Seaton, *Christmas Truce* (Pan Books, 1994) p. 68.

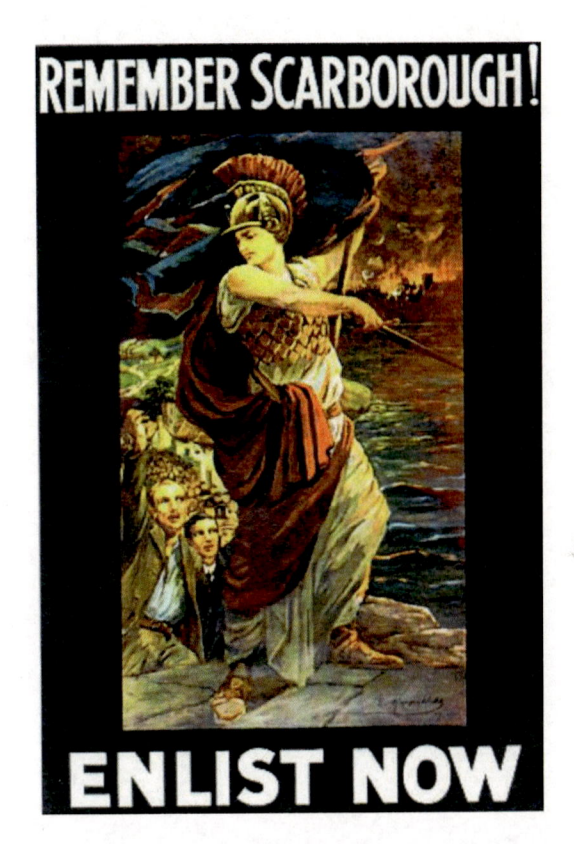

(Photo Courtesy of Scarborough Library)

Assembling horses for the Army, Cheadle Market Place, August 1914
(Photo Courtesy of George Short)

Recruits having a meal at Cheadle Station before Departure, September 1914.
(Photo Courtesy of George Short)

Millicent, Duchess of Sutherland (seated) with Members of her Medical Team at Namur
(Photo from the Author's Collection)

7

ENLISTED

By the beginning of 1915 it could be said that the general public in Britain was feeling the effects of war without actually leaving the country. Following the earlier bombardment of targets on the east coast in December by the German navy, January witnessed the first of many bombing raids on the country by German Zeppelin airships. In Staffordshire, an early system of air-raid warnings was introduced utilising buzzers or sirens of local collieries. These would give a specified number of blasts immediately a warning was received of *'approaching danger from aircraft.'* All householders were then to remain indoors and extinguish all lights. In addition, on hearing the warnings, members of Fire Brigades, Special Constables and those skilled in ambulance work were to report to local fire stations, etc. In the following month, a U-boat blockade of Britain was announced in which any shipping entering an area of water surrounding Britain and Ireland became liable to attack. The situation brought home the fact that the war was no longer confined to battles on the continent.

Meanwhile in Cheadle, Charles Masefield continued to be engaged in the day to day affairs of Blagg, Son & Masefield. Although happy in family life at 'Hanger Hill', and in his work at the Church Terrace offices, he began to feel that his duty lay elsewhere and nothing was going to persuade him otherwise.

One day in the hallway of the busy legal practice, when in conversation with Senior Partner C. J. Blagg, Charles was overheard to say *'I think Sir I ought to go.'* Blagg replied, 'Yes, *if it was me, my boy, I would go.'* He was then 82 years of age! [1] As Arthur St. John Adcock subsequently wrote, *'under whatever premonitions may have come to him, the one conviction that Charles Masefield carried with him, and that made him indifferent to what might happen to him was that - 'Right is right, and we shall prevail'.'* [2] This statement concludes the poem **Going out to Victory** composed earlier by Charles when there was a growing threat of conflict. The composition opens with the lines *'We have heard the call that comes loud above the loudest drums...'*

It is evident that he himself had heard the call and that he was intending to respond to it. Not only that, but he was ready to sacrifice all that was dearest to him. Then, on a Sunday in March, in addressing a Young Men's Club meeting at Cheadle he said, '*Just as the war has shown us we are all Englishmen, it has shown us we are all Christians. We shall not see alike on all points, but we see that the points on which we differ are negligible beside those on which we agree...*

Are we worth fighting for? Are we worth that enormous sacrifice hourly being made for us of life and limb, of sight or speech? Let us be frank with ourselves. If this war cannot cleanse us as a nation, what will? If this war, when it ends, finds us still selfish, still greedy after our own lusts and pleasures, and forgetful of our duties towards others, we are not worth dying for. Then, so far as we are concerned, all those precious lives will have been spent in vain. There is only one thing that can justify us in accepting such a sacrifice. That is the endeavour to live after the pattern of Christ. We may falter and fail in it, but if we only endeavoured England would be a changed England'.

In the following month, further appeals to enlist were being circulated throughout the country, including a direct recruitment campaign in Staffordshire. Colonel Albert Edward Blizzard visited towns in the north of the County, including Cheadle, recruiting to form a new Battalion of the North Staffordshire Regiment. Born in Tettenhall, Blizzard was already a well known figure in the area and a highly respected officer in the Territorial Army. Later, it was said he presided over his men *'with fatherly kindness.'* [4] Blizzard's recruiting campaign was successful and the Battalion became known as the $3^{rd}/5^{th}$ North Staffords (or 'Blizzard's Mob' as it was affectionately dubbed by those who proudly served under him). In Cheadle itself, the campaign attracted a large crowd at the Wheatsheaf Inn and resulted in many men offering themselves, including Charles Masefield. On 27th April he applied for a commission in Blizzard's new Battalion, subsequently undergoing the customary medical examination at the local army medical centre in Shelton. In the meantime, references as to his 'good moral character' had been supplied by, amongst others, the Rev. Edward Stafford Carlos MA., Rector of Cheadle. The application was successful and Charles was notified that he was to be appointed to the rank of 2nd/Lieutenant. [5]

Unfortunately, any question of joining the colours was soon to be put on hold, at least temporarily. At that very moment, tragedy suddenly interrupted the well-ordered running of Blagg, Son & Masefield. On 5th May 1915 Charles J. Blagg died following a short illness of influenza and a bronchial affliction. The 'Grand Old Man of Cheadle', whom many considered might go on forever, was just short of his 83rd birthday at his death. His demise resulted in Charles being delayed in joining his regiment whilst he and his uncle, remaining partner Walter E. Blagg, attempted to put the firm's business affairs in order. Like his father, Walter Blagg was very active in the community and had served in the 4th North Staffordshire Regiment during the Boer War when he attained the rank of Captain.

Meanwhile nationally, there were horrendous reports of the sinking by the Germans of the Cunard liner Lusitania. Having set sail from New York on 1st May, she had a complement of 2,000 passengers and crew. Six days later, she was sighted off the Irish coast by a submarine and torpedoed. The liner sank within 20 minutes. Described by some of the media as *'a crime that has staggered humanity'*, the act outraged public opinion across the world, prompting many anti-German riots. All aboard the vessel were non-combatants and 1,200 were drowned.

Charles eventually joined his regiment in August 1915, at its headquarters in the requisitioned Corporation Street Schools in Stafford. Having had to re-apply for his commission, this again was successful and the rank of 2nd/Lieutenant reaffirmed. [6] In the County town the actual process of basic training or 'conditioning' of the troops commenced. Like all military training, this involved almost total surrender of personal liberty and immediate unquestioned obedience to orders. Those having enlisted were engaged to serve 24hrs a day, 7 days a week, 52 weeks in the year for an undetermined period as soldiers in a complex organisation designed to enforce the will of each and every superior on those in the lower ranks. Also, to do everything without question to a word of command. Whilst training of officers may have been different in certain aspects, 2/Lt Masefield soon found himself participating in physical training sessions on Stafford Common. In a letter dated 9th August 1915 he explained to his beloved Muriel that the Colonel *'makes the great point of officers doing exercises with the men.'* He thought that she would have been amused on observing him and others attempting to squat on their heels! *'In common with other fathers of families in the ranks'* he wrote, his muscles were beginning to *'get a bit stiff.'* The correspondence also reveals more details of military life at Stafford. For example, it discloses that his orderly woke him at 6am (or earlier), and then prepared Charles's uniform and polished his boots ready for parade at 6.20. Drill then followed for an hour on the square, before finally marching to breakfast. During that meal, Charles attended to see that men of his company received *'a sufficiency of food and that there was no waste.'* After that meal, a further parade and kit inspection took place before marching to Stafford Common for a further session of drill. At this point, *'operations were handed over to the Sgt/Major.'* Yet again, further drill was exercised in the afternoon with tea at 4.15pm. In the evenings, the officers were sometimes addressed by the Colonel on various regimental matters. Accommodation for Charles was a former schoolroom which he shared with two fellow officers. As a consequence, he viewed life in the premises as *'very public.'*

On 26th August, a 100 strong contingent from the 3rd/5th Battalion attended a fete at Trentham Gardens in aid of the Red Cross organisation. According to the following day's edition of **The Sentinel**, the men gave a full afternoon's programme including regimental sports which were performed in *'perfect weather'*. The correspondent also noted that few in attendance would have realised that the men had earlier been involved in a night exercise including a 5-mile march wearing full pack and equipment! Afterwards, prizes for the various sporting events were *'graciously'* presented by Lady Harrowby, she deputising for Lady Dartmouth who was unable to attend on account of having been notified that her son was missing in action.

The correspondent also reported that there were some 5,000 in attendance at the event including 100 wounded servicemen from the nearby Stoke War Hospital which had been established in the new children's ward and other blocks at Stoke Workhouse. Officials in charge of the hospital contingent were Major Rutherford and Miss Tisdall, the Matron. The fete concluded in the evening with dancing to the Stoke-on-Trent Military Band which had also provided '*a programme of excellent music*' throughout the afternoon. According to the report, the charity event had been organised by Mrs W. A. Bowers (wife of Charles's cousin) of Caverswall Castle.

The same edition of the newspaper featured a more unusual item appertaining to the war stating that boot manufacturers in Northampton were devoting half of their capacity to production of army boots in preparation for a winter campaign. On a lighter note, an advertisement on the front page for Hanley's Grand Theatre indicated that the '*entente cordial*' revue '***All French***' was being presented all week. The show was said to have '*an all star cast*' and performed in English with 7 scenes. The advertisement concluded with the words '*look out for the girl in the muff!*' No doubt the event would have proved a welcome distraction to any of the servicemen who were able to attend.

On the actual day of the Trentham event, the

Sentinel announced that Russia was to make awards to a number of local non-commissioned officers and men for *'gallantry and distinguished service in the field.'* The latest casualty list was also reported indicating that 21 men of the 1st/5th North Staffords were wounded, and 6 dead. The regular bulletins were a constant reminder of the war situation.

In September Charles and his Battalion moved to Belton Park near Grantham, Lincolnshire where *'all the Third Line Units of the Division were assembled.'* Built in the late 19th Century for Sir John Brownlow, Belton Park even today is regarded as a perfect English country house estate with a magnificent deer park. Its vast parkland had been used by local rifle volunteers, territorial and yeomanry units for annual camps since the 1880s. When war was declared in 1914, Lord Brownlow offered Belton Park to the military authorities and it proved to be ideal for training purposes. Also, being situated close to a main railway line this enabled a branch to be provided into the site. In due course, the camp was to hold upwards of 25,000 troops. However, its construction and the huge influx of men initially caused many problems for the authorities. Accommodation by way of tents and huts had to be provided, together with water supplies, sewage disposal and many other services. On the other hand, local traders welcomed a huge increase in trade, but struggled to meet demand for essentials such as bread.

In his first correspondence from Lincolnshire dated 28th September 1915, Charles wrote that he was sharing his accommodation with Lt. Eli Robinson.[7] Describing the nights as *'very cold'* he nevertheless indicated that their little room was *'cosy'* having the benefit of *'a splendid fire in the stove.'* He also revealed that while some officers woke early due to the low temperatures, he himself was *'fairly warm'*, having received the present of a pair of bed socks *'which arrived opportunely.'* The correspondence also gives brief details of a night exercise in which the Battalion participated, parading at 8.30pm in the moonlight with all commands *'given in whispers.'* They were then marched off to an *'appointed field'* where every man had to dig himself into *'hasty entrenchment.' 'All were tremendously keen and worked like blazes'* he wrote, and within the hour were *'quite well protected against rifle fire.'* It also transpired that Charles and his fellow officers had earlier undergone bayonet practise, charging *'with great gusto'* at sacks which were hung up, or in trenches.

Meanwhile, on the Western Front, an Anglo-French offensive in the Artois-Champagne areas was being pushed back by strong German counter-attacks. During the Battle of Loos (25th September-14th October) in which the author and poet Rudyard Kipling's son John was killed, the Commander in Chief of the BEF Sir John French withheld British reserves some 16 miles behind the front line. As a consequence, advantage could not be taken of British gains. When the reserves did finally arrive on the front line, they were too late and subsequent piecemeal attacks simply cost more British casualties. French was later replaced by Sir Douglas Haig, Commander of the British 1st Army.

Up to this time, the $1^{st}/5^{th}$ North Staffords, who had been in France since March, had not taken any part in major battles. Nevertheless, they had done their fair share of trench work and suffered considerable casualties. Initially, as with other newly arrived troops, they would have served a 'trench apprenticeship'. This would have involved learning details of how to conduct one-self in the trenches including holding and relieving of them. However, on 13th October, they were involved in an attack on a strategic position - the Hohenzollern Redoubt - which lay in a series of trenches between the La Bassee Canal and Grenay near Lens. It was situated on a gentle rise with a clear field of fire before it, and reinforced with trenches containing numerous deadly machine gun emplacements. According to the ***Sentinel***, the men of the Staffords advanced with the battle cry of '*Potters for ever*' but before they had gone very far, merciless enemy machine gun fire had commenced. Men were continually falling, but their comrades pressed on. According to a War Correspondent '*the advance was magnificent*' but of the 700 officers and men who went into the attack, over 500 were killed. The terrible losses subsequently cast a sad gloom over North Staffordshire with almost every district being affected.

By this time, the $2^{nd}/5^{th}$ North Staffords had sent out several drafts to France and became a permanent unit, and it then fell to the $3^{rd}/5^{th}$ Battalion to supply reinforcements. At Belton Park a number of BEF men arrived who had returned from the Front on account of sickness or having been wounded. Eventually there was sufficient to form a Company. These men were seen as objects of awe and admiration to others, having actually experienced fighting. They remained in the country until classed as fit, and then sent out again with other drafts. The $3^{rd}/5^{th}$ Battalion immediately prepared its first draft and 18 officers and men were dispatched to Rouen to join the $1^{st}/5^{th}$. From this point onwards until the end of the war, drafts were continually being sent out.

On 7th December Charles Masefield wrote that he was in charge of a draft which was ready '*to the last bootlace*' to move at a moment's notice. Unfortunately, he then discovered a case of '*spotted fever*' in 'A' Company, '*hustled round the doctor*' and isolated them. Acting as Adjutant, he then got 'C' Company '*hard at work*' to replace them after having been '*passed fit by the doctor.*' On reporting the matter to Division, they considered that '*we have done rather a smart performance in getting 38 new men ready.*' The correspondence also reveals that, later in the day, at 7pm he received a wire from the War Office instructing that the replacement draft was to leave by special train from Grantham at 6.30am on the following morning. This operation was carried out in the rain and *'pitch dark'* conditions. The next letter from Charles was dated 15th December and addressed from the Officers' Mess, at the Embarkation Camp, Southampton. In this he reveals that on arrival at the port, they were given instructions to march the 3 miles to the billets. Having settled the men in, he then found his own accommodation in the Officers' Mess. Perhaps surprisingly, he also disclosed that he found all the officials at Southampton as *'most helpful and friendly - astonishingly free from red tape!'*

Two days later, Charles wrote a further letter from Southampton informing his son that he hoped to be home *'in a few days'*. Addressing Geoffrey as *'you old thing'*, he promised that the two would then *'do drill together'* indicating that they would be 'playing' soldiers. Having by this time supervised the embarkation of 'C' Company, he returned to Belton Park but was fortunate to be granted leave to spend Christmas with his wife and son at 'Hanger Hill.' They, in turn, would also have joined in the customary family festive celebrations at 'Rosehill' - his parents' residence.

Meanwhile, those at home in North Staffordshire had not forgotten the *'lads at the Front'* and following an appeal by Councillor Gradwell Goodwin, the Mayor of Newcastle-under-Lyme, a Christmas dinner was provided and sent out to the troops in France. According to the regiment's official history, *'the dinner was a great success, consisting of tinned turkey and tongue, and no-one wanted any tea.'* [8]

Back on the Western Front, the narrow unbroken line of trenches now stretched from the North Sea to the Swiss border wending its way around farms and chateaux, the edges of woods and across fields and meadows. Throughout 1915, the British and French armies had attempted to break through the German lines, determined to drive the enemy troops from north eastern France and Belgium. However by December, that line virtually remained in the same position as it did at the beginning of the year.

Notes

1. Ex. information Michael Collis.
2. *For Remembrance* (Hodder & Stoughton) p. 129.
3. Quoted by A. St. John Adcock in foreword to Charles Masefield, *Poems* (Oxford: Blackwell, 1919) p. 6.
4. Lt. Walter Meakin. *Op.cit*, p. 42.
5. Regimental records (PRO): copies in author's collection.
6. *Ibid.*
7. Lt.E. Robinson was killed at Gommecourt on 2nd July 1916.
8. Lt. Walter Meakin. *Op.cit*, pp. 43 - 44.

*Four Generations of the Blagg Family Photo (from left – right) C.J. Blagg, Charles Masefield with son Geoffrey & Susan Masefield.
(Photo Courtesy of Robin Masefield)*

A rare early photograph of Albert Edward Blizzard seen here as Captain in the 1St Volunteer Battalion, North Staffordshire Regiment (Photo Courtesy of Richard Masefield)

Corporation Street School, Stafford (Photographed in 1914, where Charles Masefield & his Comrades were accommodated on Enlistment) (Photo Courtesy of Roy Lewis Collection)

Belton Camp, Grantham
(Photo Courtesy of Lincolnshire Archives)

Barrack Room at Belton Camp
(Photo Courtesy of Lincolnshire Archives)

London, November 1915
Recruiting March by the King's Royal Rifle Corps
(Postcard from the Author's Collection)

Sharing a picnic with Muriel & Geoffrey during a leave period
(Photo Courtesy of Robin Masefield)

8

THE BULLRING & THE TRENCHES

According to contemporary records, the winter of 1915/16 on the Western Front was fairly quiet. Neither side attempted to break through, but instead concentrated on maintaining their trenches in 'proper condition' in anticipation of a Spring offensive. By now, methods of trench warfare had changed with the introduction of hand bombs and trench mortars. Also, there had been an enormous addition to the artillery, and in the skies over Flanders aircraft were playing more important roles, including provision of photography for pinpointing enemy positions. The winter also passed quietly at Belton Park. However, there was much mud and the camp became *'very uncomfortable'* as a consequence of its hasty construction having resulted in the site not being *'laid out for bad weather'*. [1]

On 9th February 1916, Charles Masefield wrote his last letter from Belton Park, informing Muriel that the 3rd/5th Battalion was relocating to Long Eaton, a small lace making town in Nottingham. However, domestic affairs were clearly also on his mind, particularly redecoration of 'Hanger Hill', the matter clearly having been raised by his wife in earlier correspondence. He responded by indicating that he had wanted for some time to distemper the hall and passages, but thought that he would *'wait until the house was our own'* and then do it *'really well with dados of sorts.'* The letter also confirms that he was already dealing with *'the option to buy.'* As it happened, the Battalion was to have only a brief stay at Long Eaton, it being on the move again, having received orders to relocate to Catterick Bridge, Yorkshire.

At the beginning of the war, Britain's maritime supremacy had remained unchallenged for a century or so. Some had expected another naval battle of the measure of Trafalgar, and this was to eventually occur on 31st May with the Battle of Jutland involving some 250 vessels. It was the largest battle of the war and because there was no submarine action, it has remained the biggest surface only encounter in the years since.[2] Some historians might assess the result of the battle as a draw due to the fact that the Royal Navy failed to destroy its

German naval adversary. On the other hand, the Germans claimed Jutland as a victory which was certainly true in terms of losses inflicted. The British lost 13 vessels and had a total of 6094 men killed, whilst German losses were 11 vessels and 2551 killed. However, the German fleet suffered considerable damage, and failed to break the British blockade. [3] For the rest of the war the German High Seas Fleet remained in its ports and was no longer a decisive factor. Its failure to defeat the British at sea left the Royal Navy masters of the English Channel. Advantage was taken of this situation, and urgently required reinforcements were thus able to cross to France without resistance. Numbered among these in June was the $3^{rd}/5^{th}$ Battalion, including newly promoted Lt. Charles Masefield, who eventually found themselves at Rouen. Here they received 'hard training' in the so called 'Bull Ring', an area sited on sand where both officers and men were put through arduous courses before being entrained in 'cattle trucks' up the line. There were a number of these particular training grounds, the most notorious being at Etaples. One noteworthy criticism of the 'Bull Rings' was that the 'special' instructors, usually hard type NCOs, had rarely, if at all, experienced being in any action and under fire. Officers were not exempt from the courses, they in particular being given *'final instructions on how to kill the Boches!'* The official regimental history records that Lt. C. J. B. Masefield attended one of the courses before entraining for the Front. [5]

On 3rd July, writing from *'somewhere in France'* (due to censorship of the Army which would not allow Allied plans, names of Battalions, or places etc to be named), Charles informed his *'dearest most beloved'* Muriel of the Battalion being *'cut up again'* and that his cousin, 2nd/Lt. William Aubrey Bowers had been *'seriously wounded.'* The action had taken place at Gommecourt on the previous day, resulting in heavy casualties. In fact, seven officers had been killed, including Bowers, five wounded, and casualties amongst other ranks numbered 300.[6] Charles also described marching 8 miles *'with all of us carrying full packs and equipment'* and having *'steel helmets served out en route.'* The North Staffords, in effect, took over a line of trenches a few miles south west of Arras and a few miles north of Gommecourt, and were in view of the ruined village of Ransart which was occupied by the Germans. The correspondence then continues by portraying the indescribable *'misery of the trenches'* which they had taken over - *'water generally up to your middle, sometimes for a mile.'* Those relieved from the trenches *'all looked less like men than some monstrous creatures born of mud, so coated and covered with it they were.'* The letter then closes with the comment that they were *'kept awake by shells'* and that, perhaps understandably, he is *'too sick about it all to write more today.'*

   The poet, novelist and critic Robert Graves was also one who experienced and wrote about life and conditions in the trenches. Having served as a Captain in the Royal Welch (sic) Fusiliers, he subsequently recalled *'the wet and slippery trenches'* running through the dull red clay. He also recollected seeing in torch light, hundreds of field mice and frogs which had fallen into the trenches and unable to find a way out. *'The light dazzled them'* he wrote, and *'I could not help treading on them.'* [7] Graves also wrote of casualties from 'trench foot', observing that a Battalion of dismounted cavalry at

Bouchavesnes on the Somme *'lost half its strength in two days from trench feet.'* [8] At one period it was a crime to get trench foot, but it is understood that no humane commander enforced the penalty. In his classic account of life on the Western Front, Graves also notes that he found it necessary at times to run his thumb nails up the seams of shirts to kill lice. Lice were said to be the cause of the spread of 'trench fever'. Rats were also a constant problem, he recalled, coming from nearby canals, etc. They would frequently arrive at night-time in the dug-outs and trenches, finding their way into bedding as the men attempted to sleep. [9] Some found that they were unable to bear the conditions of the trenches and a few resorted to suicide or deserted.[10] As for Robert Graves himself, the dehumanising horrors of the war left him shell-shocked, and they haunted him for the rest of his life.

On 5th July 1916, Charles continued the regular correspondence to his wife. Writing from the front line he disclosed that *'we are in the peculiar position of being unable to see the Boches'* (slang for German, also spelt Bosche) *front line, as we are on the crest of a rise, and*

Fritz down in the hollow below us. So what you see when you look over the parapet is merely a luxuriant growth of thistles and barbed wire for 10, 20 & 40 yds, and then nothing until, on the other side of the hollow 400yds away, you see Fritz's second and third lines, barbed wire, etc. All I have seen of Fritz so far is one periscope which happened to catch the sun yesterday morning. A man next to me took a shot at it, down it went like lightning... All we do really at the moment is to hold our line secure.'

The letter continues *'when the weather is fine the life is really not at all bad, but yesterday afternoon it rained hard and in a few moments reduced the trenches to a quagmire. There is a sea of yellow mud everywhere, all over your clothes and hands, in the water you wash in (when you do wash!) and standing water all over the floor of the dug-out I'm writing in. You sleep in your boots always of course and never take off your revolver. I slept last night with feet wet through but feel not a penny the worse. The men are wonderful. Their lives are several degrees wretcheder than ours, of course, when it rains, yet I haven't heard one grouse yet...'*

The weather was certainly the subject of one of the

songs sung by the troops at the time. Sung to the air of ***Holy, Holy, Holy,*** the words are:

'Raining, raining, raining,
Always bloody-well raining,
Raining all the morning,
And raining all the night...

Constant traffic up and down communication trenches did turn them into quagmires when it rained. The incessant downpours also, at times, caused trench sides to collapse, as did enemy shelling. But those in the trenches were also fearful of losing their way in the dark and straying from the duckboards, then slipping and being sucked into the swampy conditions. Consequently, whilst some would have preferred to have been fighting instead of being unable to participate in an attack because of the appalling conditions, others would pray for the rain to continue until there was no longer any chance of an order from High Command which could amount to a pointless advance.

Further details of the appalling conditions in the trenches are revealed in a letter dated 10th July to son Geoff. *'In the trenches we have too much water very often,'* he wrote, *'it keeps your feet wet and the men are wet through.'* He continued, *'it is the same for the Germans. After a wet night we can see them sometimes baling water out of their trenches. It would be much nicer for everybody if we could only agree with them to fight in nice dry places!'* He also comments on the frequency of aircraft seen - *'so often we don't bother to look at them.'* These had provided photographs of the German trenches *'dug in white chalk, so they show up very well.'* The letter concludes with the note that they were expecting to return to the trenches on the following night - *'going in after dark so that the Germans can't see us coming along the road.'*

During this period, the Rev'd G. A. Studdert Kennedy was attached to the Brigade as Chaplain. Otherwise known as 'Woodbine Willie', he frequently visited the men in the trenches, carrying a large cardboard box containing packets of cigarettes which he distributed. Studdert Kennedy was very popular and when rumours went around that 'Woodbine Willie' was on his rounds, morale was boosted. The chaplain would go into the firing line to help attend the wounded, and even assist with digging and other tasks. His direct language appealed to the men and there was always good attendances when he preached on Sundays.[11] As chaplains were ranked as officers, it is just possible that Charles Masefield may have met Studdert Kennedy and other members of the clergy in the environs of the mess, or as they went about their pastoral duties. They were part of the army structure but separate from it, possessing their own reporting lines and, as some would point out, had a direct line to the Highest Authority of them all! They were generally respected for their moral and spiritual qualities, but even more so when they showed courage under fire. In addition to administering to the spiritual needs of their flock, some of the army chaplains would assist with stretcher bearing, etc., but when out of the line could also be seen participating in social activities such as a game of football. Chaplains preached the gospel of self-sacrifice. There are instances of soldiers being baptised on the field, and on the eve of key offensives chaplains would find their oft-makeshift church full to bursting. Writing in the biography of his grandfather, Peter Fiennes wrote that '*we can assume that many of the men listening to the chaplain* on a Church Parade Service would have been indifferent...but there would have been many more who were actively engaged or possibly welcoming the diversion and thanking God they weren't up the line!' [12]

Surprisingly, horror and humour mingled inexplicably on the western Front. Evidence of this is ***The Somme Times*** (initially ***The Wipers Times)***, copies of which survive. A satirical newspaper, it answered the troops' need for light relief with a remarkable stream of hilarious invention and humour. Said to have acted as the voice of the average British soldier, the newspaper was a satire of life on the Western Front. As Ian Hislop wrote in his introduction to the complete recently reprinted series – '*it is quite literally laughing in the face of death, with jokes about flamethrowers and gas attacks from the troops who were facing them. It is also very rude about senior officers, the Home Front and the organisation of war.*' [13] Anyone who has had an opportunity of reading this extraordinary publication would agree that it was ahead of its time, and almost a prototype of ***Private Eye*** magazine. Its material was actually written and proof checked in the trenches and then printed on an abandoned printing press salvaged from the ruins of Ypres ('Wipers' to the British troops!).

Of necessity, the newspaper title changed as its editors moved around the Western Front, it eventually becoming the *The BEF Times*. Also, this gave no indication to the Germans where they might be based, should copies fall into their hands. In addition to original verse, parodies of popular poems of the time were included. Even Rudyard Kipling's *If* was not above being 're-crafted', this version being featured in the edition of 1st November 1917 –

'If you can drink the beer the Belgians sell you,
And the price they ask with ne'er a grouse,
If you believe the tales that some tell you
And live in mud with ground sheet for a house…
If you can grin at last when handing over,
And finish well what you have begun,
And think a muddy ditch a bed of clover,
You'll be a soldier one day, then, my son!'

Fabricated advertisements were a regular popular feature, the following from the edition of 3rd July 1916 being a typical example -

'Is your dug-out in a dangerous position? We will insure it for you at a small charge'.

Yet another example of trench humour is featured in the edition of 31st July 1916. In this, correspondence purporting to be from Ornithologists Grandpa & Nickett, claims that they have been successful in crossing a parrot with a pigeon! They are hoping that the resultant 'Parrotidgin' will eventually be of immense use to the War Office, as the bird can deliver its message by word of mouth! The final page of the newspaper states that it was *'Printed and published by Sherwood, Forester & Co., Ltd. 'Sommewhere'* (Sic) *in France.'*

At the time of this particular edition, it is unquestionable that the situation of his Company may be described as dire, but whether Charles Masefield actually shared this style of humour or even saw a copy of the newspaper is uncertain. Writing to Colonel Blizzard on 13th August from the trenches, he indicates that *'we are very short of officers'* and the need for more drafts as *'the total strength of this company at the present moment is*

86.'* This was as a result of having dug an advanced trench *'50yds or so of the present front line of C & D Companies'* many were killed or wounded from enemy machine gun fire. The weather had been very hot for three weeks or so, but Charles informed the Colonel that this was *'better than rain in the trenches.'* A fellow officer in his correspondence wrote home describing the sky at night as being lit up *'by flashes'* which reminded him of home and the dramatic sight when the mighty blast furnace opened at the Shelton Bar Steelworks.

On 17th August, Charles wrote that he had shot a partridge with the aid of his revolver - *'a sitting shot, needless to say! We had him for dinner tonight, a very welcome change from the eternal beef. There are a lot about No Man's Land, where of course they have a very peaceful existence among the rank grass and thistle.'* Surprisingly, troops in Flanders received an amount of food parcels from home to supplement their army fare. Among the contents were the very popular traditional North Staffordshire oatcake.[14] Fowl, sausages, and pies were also despatched from the County to its sons serving on the Western Front, but dependent on where intended recipients were when mail arrived, the items were not always in good condition or perhaps even edible. Charles Masefield's correspondence reveals that he very much appreciated receiving *'cake and rocky buns.'* Also to keep abreast of local news he loved to receive copies of the **Weekly Sentinel**.

The services of the Post Office were crucial to both communications and the war effort during hostilities. In the period 1915-16 alone, the Annual Report of the Postmaster General reveals that some 10 million letters and 700,000 parcels weekly were being despatched to the troops. Soft fruit could also be sent in the post to the Front providing it was packed in special metal boxes with tightly fitting lids *'in such a way that the juice cannot exude'* and marked *'Fruit with care'*. To handle the huge quantity of mail and additional services such as the nation's telegraph and telephone services, the Post Office at this time employed over 350,000. It was the biggest economic enterprise in Britain, and the largest single employer of labour in the world. [15]

Maintaining his own personal regular correspondence, on 1st September 1916 Charles wrote to his beloved Muriel *'from one of the forts behind the line.'* Addressing her as *'my heart's delight'*, he informed her during that morning he had been conducting a squad in gas drill when through a gap in the hedge *'a most resplendent figure suddenly appeared followed by an almost splendid staff subaltern. He proved to be no less a person that the GOC Army Corps. He asked what I was doing. I said being useful and he passed on his majestic way!'* Charles admitted that he didn't even know his name! In the same letter he also told Muriel that he would appreciate receiving more reading material and particularly requested a copy of Arnold Bennett's **Helen With The High Hand.** Turning to the subject of the weather, he revealed that conditions had improved and that he had *'lightened his valise by the drastic act of jettisoning two blankets - leaving only my flea bag!'* Finally, he wrote that he expected to go up to the trenches that night, *'but there's little danger about that now.'* Nonetheless, having said that, he added *'the other night after dinner, we had a stray bullet bang through the front door of the billet!'*

On 5th September in a further letter *'from the

trenches,' Muriel was informed that he thought that he had *'accounted for his first Boche'* on the previous afternoon. Apparently, a Forward Observation Officer (FOO) in the trenches had informed him that with the aid of his *'very excellent telescope'* he had spotted a Boche sentry. Having confirmed this, Charles borrowed a rifle and fired at the unsuspecting target, whereupon the FOO reported that the sentry had *'dropped like a stone.'* Shortly afterwards the Germans *'suddenly began sniping furiously'* at the point he had fired from, sending *'about 40 bullets in return for my one.'* The letter also discloses a change in the weather to *'heavy rain-pretty beastly.'* Having captured some prisoners, they had also learned that *'a fresh lot of the enemy'* were facing them.

A perhaps rare contemporary timetable of an officers' life in the trenches is given to Muriel on 7th September. Writing in his usual clear hand, Charles details his activities as follows -

7.15pm. (last night) Had an excellent dinner of soup, fried beef with cabbage & tinned beans and pineapple chunks.
8.00pm. 'Stood to' i.e. every officer mans the trench for an hour to repel attack.

9.00pm. Went out with a party of 12 men into No Man's Land through a gap in our wire and lay down in ambush for any Boche who might be on the move. We returned at 11.30pm having seen nobody. The Boche is suffering a good deal from nerves and we were again amused last night by the spectacle of him throwing bombs into his own wire under the quite mistaken impression that some of us were there.

12.15am. Got to bed.

4.15am. Wakened to stand to. Thick mist over the Boche lines. Had a stroll with a fellow officer inspecting newly erected barbed wire.

5.45am. Breakfast - bacon and toasted cheese, tea and jam.

6.30am. On duty in trench. Spotted a Boche through my glasses looking through his and smoking a pipe...had a couple of shots at him but the range (1,000yds) was too great. Also spotted behind the Boche lines the wreckage of an aeroplane brought down last night - ours I feel.

9.00am. Come off duty - sleep for 3 hours.

And so the war goes on' he wrote.

The letter concludes '*we are living like lords.*

Mother sent a cake, rocky buns, gingerbread and oatmeal biscuits - an ideal collection.' Generally, in the back areas, rations were plentiful with Quartermasters indenting for the strength of the whole Battalion, as it might be before going into action. But in the actual firing line it was a different matter where one might be fortunate to receive a regular supply of tinned food. Also if a convoy of supplies were held up for various reasons, there could be disastrous results.

Meanwhile, while there had been some success in slowly pushing the Germans back, it was clear that in the trench warfare that existed on the Western Front, cavalry had become obsolete in the face of the machine gun. A new tactic was essentially required such as 'an armoured horse' or 'land battleship' which was capable of negotiating the trenches, whilst also resisting the piercing bullets of the machine guns. This was to appear in the Battle of Flers-Courcellette on 15th September 1916. The secret new weapon in the form of a heavily armoured car (or tank) enabled the capture by New Zealand troops of the village of Flers. Thirty two of the new 'armoured monsters' were committed, trampling over machine gun emplacements and killing the enemy with deadly fire, the infantry then following on for 'mopping up' operations. Although not perfect and perhaps at that stage not the wonder weapon hoped for, the prototype tank, nevertheless, had demonstrated its potential to break the trench warfare deadlock.

The British troops continued to push forward across the muddy wastes bringing a new optimism that the war was nearing a conclusion. But as war correspondent Philip Gibbs wrote at the end of September - '*it is only the beginning. People at home must not think that the German army has lost its power of defence and that the great rout is at hand. They are drawing back their guns, but saving most of them. They are retreating, but will still stand again, and dig new trenches and defend other villages. There will be greater and fiercer and more desperate fighting before the end comes, and God alone knows when that will be.*' [16]

Notes

1. Lt. Walter Meakin, *op.cit*, p. 48.
2. Victoria Carolan, *WWI at Sea* (Pocket Essentials 2007) p. 99.
3. *Ibid,* pp. 113-114.
4. Martin Gilbert, *The Somme* (John Murray, 2007) p. 29.
5. Lt. Walter Meakin, *op.cit,* p. 64.
6. *Ibid,* p.61.
7. *Goodbye to All That* (Penguin Books, 1960) p. 97.
8. *Ibid,* p. 180.
9. *Ibid,* pp. 142-143.
10. *Ibid,* p. 106.
11. Lt. Walter Meakin, *op.cit,* p. 67.
12. Peter Fiennes, *To War with God* (Mainstream Publishing Co, 2011) p. 71.
13. *The Wipers Times* (Little Books Ltd, 2009) p. vii.
14. Ted Riley in letter to his mother. 24 Nov 1916 (copy in author's collection).
15. Information kindly provided by the British Postal Museum & Archive.
16. Philip Gibbs, *The Battles of the Somme* (Heineman, 1917) p. 302.

A Typical Example of a "Sweetheart" or Separation Postcard which were Sent Home by Soldiers during World War I
(Postcard from Author's Collection)

A Typical Example of a World War I Postcard depicting Trench Humour whilst at the same time sending Christmas Greetings
(Postcard from Author's Collection)

Postal Delivery to Soldiers on the Western Front in winter during WWI
(Photo Courtesy of the British Postal Museum & Archive)

Women Sorters Repacking Broken Parcels for the Troops during WWI
(Photo Courtesy of the British Postal Museum & Archive)

Training at the Notorious Bullring at Etaples
(Photo from Author's Collection)

Men of the Staffordshire Regiment reading by Candlelight in the Trenches
(Photo Courtesy of the Imperial War Museum REF: Q1556)

9

SPECIAL LEAVE

As shock waves continued to vibrate across the world about the worsening conflict and alleged German atrocities, the Allies began a new offensive on 1st October 1916. However, heavy rain fell during the first few days making the mud of Picardy sticky and deep, resulting in the movement of heavy armament more difficult and a consequent reduction in the number of artillery barrages. But the British continued to inch forward and by 7th October, the key town of Le Sars had been captured. A series of light railways had also been constructed by this period, which improved transportation of the vast quantity of various supplies required.

Meanwhile, following an attack of trench fever, Charles Masefield had spent a short period in No.14 General Hospital at Wimereux near Boulogne. He appears to have been fortunate in having only a mild bout, as for some having suffered from the condition their fighting days were over. The hospital, being the Hotel

Splendide in peacetime, was situated on the seafront next door to a casino. It was an officers' hospital of 200 beds and had a constantly changing population. The maximum number of officers admitted on one night, and when action occurred, was about 80. By the following night, half of that number would be on their way to England and another convoy would have brought new patients to fill the beds which had been vacated. According to a nurse who had served there at the time, *'the hotel adapted itself very well to the needs of an officers' hospital.'* The entrance hall and corridors were large and airy with good oak furniture and screens. Large palms, plants and fresh flowers adorned the tables. The lounge with all the latest newspapers and comfortable chairs, together with the dining room, led to a covered-in balcony which overlooked the sea. From this, on clear days, the cliffs of Dover could be seen. When the weather was at its best, the windows would be flung open to let in the sun and air.

The nurse recalled the occasions when ambulances arrived steadily through the night, each *'disgorging'* its load of wounded - *'men who were once smart, well-turned out British officers, but who now to all* outward appearance, were absolute ruffians, plastered with mud, their coats in rags, and often wearing scrubby beards.' At such times, to the uninitiated, the place would have appeared *'a regular maze of wounded men, stretchers and kits'* through which medical staff instinctively found their way. But, being a military establishment, everything was thoroughly organised from the time of arrival when *'the energetic sergeant at the front door superintended the transport of wounded men on stretchers'* into the building, until subsequently when the same wounded personnel, then labelled with all their particulars, were transferred to a hospital ship for 'Blighty' (as the men referred to home).[1] To most of the troops on the Western Front to receive 'a blighty one' (or wound) was a hope and dream which, if it happened, resulted in being openly envied. Strange as this may appear, many men at times also felt ready to lose an arm or leg in exchange for a permanent return home.

    Having been discharged from hospital, Charles took two days to rejoin the Battalion which had now been merged with the $3^{rd}/6^{th}$ North Staffords under the command of Colonel Blizzard. Writing from his billet on

8th October, he disclosed that he had *'an excellent time in hospital'* at Wimereux where *'they feed you quite on Hotel Splendide lines.'* There had been *'quite a number of mothers and children'* at the resort while he had been there, *'bathing regularly for the weather was wonderfully warm.'* He added that they also had been amusing themselves *'in queer French ways like playing croquet on the rather shingly beach!'*

On a more serious note, Charles wrote that the Battalion had *'experienced an interesting time'* in his absence. They had raided the enemy trenches one night, he explained, killing about eight Boches without any loss. As a consequence, two officers were to receive the Military Cross. Subsequently, the Boche had paid them two return visits, the first being a complete failure, *'leaving a dead man behind them.'* However, on the second occasion, they had rushed the trench and managed to take a prisoner back with them. Concluding the letter, he noted that *'the mud season has now set in in earnest.'*

On the following day Charles informed his wife that he was *'just off to the trenches…it is fine but I shall be greatly surprised if we don't have a pretty wet tour.'* At this time each tour of the trenches was for 4 days, after which they were relieved by the 6th North Staffords. Rest billets were situated in the villages of Berles-au-Bois and Bailleumont. [2]Charles's correspondence of 9th October does not disclose the actual location of the billets due to normal censorship, but he discloses that he and the men are at a farm with '*a gateway from the street into the farmyard in which the most prominent object is the manure heap occupying the centre. The house stands on the far side of it, and on either side are farm buildings of mud and lath. The best of them are occupied by our men. We officers,*' he continued, '*always live in the parlour which invariably has a big stove and a big oaken sideboard, a table and a few chairs - that's all. The family, if there is one, lives in the house place sleeping in a huge box bed. In one of the stables at his billet is a printed card to a certain saint to preserve us and our beasts from accidents and maladies.*' He also comments that at the other village where they were billeted alternatively, there were '*very few civilians left*' but every now and then '*the Boche takes it into his head to shell it and some of the houses have gaping holes in them.*' His poem ***Candle-light*** gives a delightful sketch of the time spent in a French billet -

'Candle-light is so mellow and warm
When a man comes in all hungry and cold,
Clotted with mud, or wet from the storm-
Only of candle-light you shall be told.

Of Madame's brave, sad eagerness.
And French serenity of dress,
Her quiet, quick ways as she goes
To dry our heavy, sodden clothes
And bring all hot the great ragout
That makes once more a man of you,
Her pains to help us put away
The sights that we have seen all day,
Her talk of kine and oats and rye
And Francois' feats when but so high-
You'd never guess, did you not know,
He died for France three months ago.
And then there's Marthe, whom he has left
(So proud, and yet so all bereft),
And Marie, with her hair in ties,

*Looking at you with great round eyes
That make you wish to heaven you were
The hero that you seem to her.
And last and least
There's Francois' little Jean-Baptiste,
For whom, deep slumbering in his cot,
All wounds and wars and deaths are not.
Such is the household every night
Illuminated by the candle-light.*

*Search-lights are so blinding and white
The things they show you shall not hear,
Enough to see them; it is not right
We should tell of them too, my love, my dear.'*

Subsequent correspondence of 17th October reveals that Charles and his men were resting in billets in the village of Berles-au-Bois which had been shelled *'by Fritz.'* *'As it is possible that he may do so again at any moment'* he explained, *'the men all have to sleep in caves cut out of the chalk, and we are in cellars. Our cellar isn't at all a bad bedchamber - pretty dry, and we have moved our wire netting mattresses down into it.'*

From time to time various prominent and distinguished figures visited the troops at the Front for diverse reasons. Of these, undoubtedly the most important were King George V and Edward, Prince of Wales. Other visitors included high level statesmen Herbert Henry Asquith (then Prime Minister); David Lloyd George (then Secretary of State for War); Winston Churchill (then Minister for Munitions); and Arthur James Balfour (then First Lord of the Admiralty). Perhaps surprisingly, certain entertainment performers of the day were also allowed to visit the men, even at the Front. One of these was the music hall star Harry Lauder (later Sir) who, for a short time, helped the weary soldiers to temporarily forget the horrors of war and the trenches as he joked and sang, backed by a small number of musicians. The novelist Arnold Bennett also visited the battlefields, as did Charles's kinsman John, although the two members of the Masefield family are unlikely to have met. After all, there was a war on!

In the case of John Masefield, the by now famous author and poet was a guest on 18th October at Val Vion, Beauquesnes, some 10 miles behind the front line. This was the chateau headquarters of General Sir Douglas Haig, Commander in Chief of the BEF. Earlier, John Masefield had served with the British Red Cross in the Dardanelles campaign after which he wrote **Gallipoli,** said to be one of the finest accounts of modern warfare. When published in 1916, *'it sold like wildfire'* according to his biographer.[3] Word of the book spread quickly across the Channel, as a consequence of which he received *'a pressing invitation'* to meet Haig with a view to him writing a *'Chronicle'* of the Somme. As an inducement, he would be given a Commission, a car placed at his disposal, together with a guide, maps and *'every facility.'* [4] This eventually resulted in the publication of his books **The Old Front Line** in 1917 and later **The Battle of the Somme** in 1919. *'What it was like cannot be imagined by those who were not there'* he wrote, commenting on the stupefying chaos of the endless days of attack and counter attack, not to mention the squalor of mud and rain in the trenches. Having also observed men making their way to the Front Line at night he noted - *'here and there, in recesses in the trench, under roofs of corrugated iron covered with sandbags, they* *passed the offices and the stores of war, telephonists, battalion headquarters, dumps of bombs, barbed wire, rockets, lights, machine gun ammunition, tins, jars and cases. Many men, passing these things as they went 'in' for the first time, felt with a sinking feeling of the heart, that they were leaving all ordered and arranged things, perhaps forever, and that the men in charge of these stores enjoyed by comparison, a life like a life at home.'* [5] In some sectors, men even passed rows of coffins. Nevertheless, after all such comments, he lived in the hope that *'this war will someday end, and the ruins will be rebuilt and the field of death will grow food and all this frontier of trouble will be forgotten...'* [6]

On the Home Front, there was a crisis situation in the offices of Blagg, Son & Masefield in Cheadle following the death on 27th October 1916 of Walter Edward Blagg. Charles's uncle was the last of the Blagg dynasty at the family practice and held the position of Senior Partner.[7] Like his father, he was very active in the life of the community, a sidesman at the Parish Church and held directorships in a number of local companies. In addition, he was Registrar and High Bailiff of Cheadle

County Court and became Clerk to Cheadle Magistrates on his father's retirement from the post. A member of the Parish Council since its inception, he served as Vice-Chairman for 14 years and also represented the town on Staffordshire County Council. With his wife Beatrice, Walter Blagg resided at 'Hill Crest' opposite the Masefield's 'Rosehill' at Town End. On his death, the ***Cheadle & Tean Times*** mourned his loss, commenting that '*he left behind a bright example of goodness.*' [8]

On being notified of Walter's death Charles, then being the sole family survivor of the law practice, applied to demobilise. Not surprisingly, this was refused, but the War Office did grant special leave whereupon he was at least temporarily reunited with his loving family. Writing from his home 'Hanger Hill' on 26th November, he told Colonel Blizzard of the '*great shock*' on learning of Walter's death from Bright's disease. He explained that he had been granted 2 months leave, but considered that he would have to apply for an extension as he had been appointed Clerk to the Justices and had '*innumerable matters to attend to which no-one by myself know the circumstances...Ever since I came home*' he continued,

I've been up to my neck in work, having to take up the whole work of the office at a moment's notice.' The letter concludes with the comment that he was *'very sick about having to leave the Battalion, but really there seems no help for it.'*

Meanwhile, on the Western Front, the British had continued to edge forward and captured Beaumont Hamel and Beaucort on the north bank of the Ancre. The Battle of the Somme then closed down after 4 months or so of bitter fighting. The result was the gain of a strip of muddy ground 6 miles x 20. But by this time the British and Dominion casualties alone numbered some 400,000. The only good news was that the German line had been broken. November saw a deterioration in the weather with the first snow having fallen on the battlefield and a return to the appalling conditions.

On 7th December, David Lloyd Gorge replaced Asquith as British Prime Minister. A critic of the Somme, Lloyd George was elected on the promise of a full and final victory. A few days later, as if by coincidence, the Germans invited peace negotiations, the headlines reading *'German Peace Overture.'* [9] On 14th December, the British Press was reported as being *'unanimous in asserting that no peace terms should be entertained which do not satisfy the ends for which the Allies are fighting.'* It regarded the offer as a sign of a decline of Germany's military power and a bid for neutral support in order to win a victory by diplomacy rather than by force of arms. [10] Some three days later, the newspapers reported details of the French response to the German peace initiative. Having captured Verdun, French divisions had pushed back the Germans and taken 9,000 prisoners. This was aided by French aviators working closely with the infantry *'flying over advancing lines and returning with information on the progress of attack.'* [11]

On 18th December it was announced to cheers in the House of Commons that *'men on Christmas leave from the Front would have priority over all other traffic.'* [12] Meanwhile, as the curtain was also about to rise on the festive season in North Staffordshire, the **Sentinel** was heralding local events including Hanley's Theatre Royal pantomime 'Jack and the Beanstalk' starring *'the wondrous Fairy Dreadnought.'* At least for Charles Masefield and any other fellow service personnel on leave in the area, such events would prove to be a welcome relief from the horrors of the trenches, be it only temporary.

Notes

1 Eva Cicely Fox, *'An officers' Hospital in France During the War* (Unpublished account on Scarletfinders).
2 Lt. Walter Meakin, *op.cit,* p. 64.
3 Constance Babington Smith, *John Masefield in Life* (OUP, 1978) p. 159.
4 *Ibid,* p. 163.
5 John Masefield, *The Old Front Line* (Macmillan, 1917) p. 23.
6 *Ibid,* p. 9.
7 The position regarding Walter's remaining brother Ernest W. H. Blagg remains unclear. It would appear that he was not working for the family practice at this time. If he had been, then presumably Charles Masefield would not have been granted special leave. Geoffrey Masefield in his *A History of the Senior Branch of the Masefield Family* (Private publication 1975) states that Ernest '*worked in the family office for a short period'* his real interest being hunters and the dogs which he bred '*with great professional success'* (p. 31). Furthermore, the obituary published in the NSFC Transactions following Charles's death states that he was summoned

home in October 1916 following his uncle's death which left him (i.e. Charles) *the sole survivor of his firm'*, (Vol. III 1917-18, p. 109). However, there is evidence that Ernest was working as Clerk to the Justices in 1919, and therefore he could have assisted at the practice from time to time.

8   F. J. Johnson, *op.cit.* p. 151.
9   *Staffordshire Sentinel.* 13 Dec 1916.
10 *Ibid,* 14 Dec 1916.
11 *Ibid,* 17 Dec 1916.
12 *Ibid,* 18 Dec 1916.

General Sir Douglas Haig, Commander in Chief of British Forces on the Western Front (1915 – 1918)

John Edward Masefield who in later life became Poet Laureate

FIRE
your Money at the Huns

JOIN the throng of patriotic investors who all this week have been hurrying to lend their money to their country. Draw out your savings and buy War Bonds. Back up our lads at the Front with the full strength of your bank balance. Help to win our Gun.

||| THE GUN that will speak for CHEADLE

Don't delay. Every tick of your watch brings you nearer to the end of the week, nearer to the end of this great opportunity. Go to the Bank or Money Order Post Office and invest every shilling you possibly can. No sum can be too large. £15,000 are needed by Saturday. But do not think your help is not required even if you have only a few shillings to invest. Those few shillings may pay for the explosive that sends the first shell hurtling forth from our own Gun.

Buy
National War Bonds
and War Savings Certificates

No 14 General Hospital, Wimereux (Former Hotel Splendide) where Charles Masefield recovered from Trench Fever is seen to the left. (Photo from Author's Collection)

Soldiers convalescing at the City General Hospital, Newcastle under Lyme during WWI (Photo Courtesy of Newcastle Borough Museum)

10

RETREAT OF THE BOCHE

The New Year commenced with the media reporting of Kaiser Wilhelm II's angry reaction at the Allies' rejection of his peace manoeuvre and his resultant pledge that *'the war will be continued!'* [1] In response, the new Premier, David Lloyd George reaffirmed his belief that *'with proper support at hand, the gallant armies would cleave a victory during 1917...After the war, the world would be able to attend to its business in peace.'* [2]

France at this time was in the grip of frost which seemed to grow steadily more severe. The bitterly cold weather made it impossible to dig deeply into the frozen ground and improve the trench systems. The front-line men on both sides huddled against the wintry conditions, sheltering in shallow depressions on the ice bound surface with the only significant military activity being in the air. Thus, at times, if you were an infantry man shivering in a mud clogged trench, watching aerial dogfights was the only form of real activity to help you through the long frostbitten days! Some troops considered themselves fortunate in being transported towards the Front in a fleet of specially imported London buses. Whilst they may have regarded this as a form of treat, as opposed to a lengthy march, others did not appreciate the reduction in journey time through scenes of desolation to the actual war zone.

In February, the Germans began a highly organised retreat from their hard fought final line on the Somme to the newly reinforced Hindenburg Line - a deep fortified zone intended to halt any allied military breakthrough before it could approach the Belgian or German frontier. The strategic withdrawal was timed well, making use of the hard frost for the movement of men, heavy guns and equipment. In doing so, they destroyed what could not be easily taken in the withdrawal and left very little behind. In some areas a few snipers and machine gunners remained until the main forces had been withdrawn. Occasionally, the North Staffords came across fires that were still lit in some German dugouts and, in others, traps had been left in the shape of bombs with time fuses set.

Meanwhile in Cheadle, the effect of the war on local shops would not have escaped the attention of the Masefield family, nor indeed the other residents of the town. Because of food restrictions and shortage of manpower, the number of grocers and butchers shops had reduced dramatically. Initially, the Government had relied solely upon common sense and goodwill to counter food and fuel shortage. However, as a result of panic buying, a number of emergency measures were introduced. These included the setting up of Food Control Committees, a milk priority scheme and bread rationing. On the other hand, as is generally the case, certain other retailers were able to 'take advantage' of the war situation, promoting the sale of goods 'for Tommy' - soldiers on active service. The public were urged to *'buy British and kill our enemy's trade.'* Examples of presents being sent out to the troops were soft woollen helmets for the cold (being promoted by Greenwoods), socks and shirts, trench mirrors, Rodine for killing rats, and Harrison's Pomade for killing lice.[3]

On 10th February 1917, Charles Masefield left Cheadle to rejoin his regiment, leaving the family law firm in the charge of newly appointed solicitor Edward Oswald Foster. He was to devote the rest of his working life to Blagg, Son & Masefield until the practice was sold in 1945.

On the day that Charles bid a fond farewell to his family, the ***Staffordshire Sentinel*** featured an advertisement for the film 'The Battle of the Ancre and advance of the tanks' which was being shown at a number of local cinemas in the area. *'Go and see the tanks'* it urged its readers, *'follow the crews as they get ready for the fray, follow them as they cross the trenches and wander over 'No Man's Land' crushing down the German wire entanglements.'* The film would have been the first opportunity for the general public to actually see a tank in action.

Charles did not return to France at the time, but reported to Brocton Camp on Cannock Chase. Situated on the doorstep of South Staffordshire's Black Country, the vast area of protected moorland and forest was once the hunting ground of Plantagenet Kings. Brocton Coppice to the north still had some of the original great oaks remaining. Writing earlier in his famous ***Staffordshire*** volume, Charles described the Chase as a *'very charming expanse of high moorland... Its scenery is very diverse, it is a region of swelling hills parted by deep gullies, often containing pretty streamlets, and is covered in parts by bracken, in parts by heath and in other parts by pretty groves of birch and small timber, while many of the summits are crowned by fine groups of aged pines.'* He also noted that the Chase is *'the most southerly point in England on which the red grouse breeds.'* It is doubtful, however, when he was researching and writing the book that he ever imagined that the oasis of ancient forest land and heath would become a vast military training camp during World War I and that he would be participating in it. The area was said to be excellent for army training purposes by virtue of being fairly free from mud due to the strata consisting of Bunter pebble beds, unlike Flanders!

Based at the School of Instruction at Brocton Camp, Charles participated in a course with fellow officers who *'spent nearly all their time working out tactical schemes.'* In a letter dated 20th March he informed Colonel Blizzard that the work was *'very interesting.'*

However, much of the correspondence expresses at *'being sick at learning of the new lot of casualties in the poor old Battalion.'* These included Captain Arthur Felix Wedgwood and Lieutenant Thomas Edward Lewty who were killed on 14th March in an unsuccessful attack on German trenches at Bucquoy, a few miles east of Gommecourt. In leading the company, Capt. Wedgwood was shot as he attempted to cut his way through wire. Similarly, Lt. Lewty was killed as he attempted to bomb an enemy machine gun post which was holding up the attack. In that action alone, six officers had been killed, four wounded and one taken prisoner. Another officer, not of the Battalion, later wrote of *'the gallant attack'* and expressed the view that the North Staffords would have got through if anyone could. *'Captain Wedgwood died facing the enemy and cheering his men on, and no-one could have wished for a nobler death.'* [4] Charles told Col. Blizzard that *'it seems to be my fate somehow to lose almost all the fellows I liked best in the Battalion.'*

Two days after the battle, the Germans retired from Bucquoy and on 18th March the North Staffords occupied the enemy's former headquarters at

Gommecourt. Here they had the opportunity to examine the German system of defence and were said to be *'impressed'* by it - *'everything pointed to German thoroughness, the wire entanglements were absolute eye openers, for in places his wires were quite a 100yds from his front lines and were put in a series of belts quite 30yds in depth. They were almost impossible to get through in broad daylight.'*

As the German line was falling back, Haig was preparing to attack enemy positions between the mining town of Lens to the north and Arras to the south. The British offensive began on Easter Monday 9th April following a preliminary heavy bombardment. To the right was the Canadian Division facing Vimy Ridge, an important point some 20 miles north of the Somme. The Canadians were not only successful in storming the ridge, but they managed to establish a line beyond it. However, the cost was high with some 10,000 casualties including 4,000 dead, which resulted in British generals taking the unprecedented step of protesting to Haig who actually concurred. Some 4,000 German prisoners were taken in the action, but from here, the battle slowed down with few gains. A 4-mile gap which had been created in the German line on the first day was not fully exploited by the British and soon plugged with German reinforcements. Weather conditions were atrocious with frequent snowstorms interrupted by either sleet or rain. This further hampered advances and on 15th April, Haig ordered an end to the offensive. However, a week earlier America officially joined the war against Germany and this was a great boost to allied morale.

Back in England, Charles Masefield had by this time rejoined Colonel Blizzard and the Battalion, now located at Lincoln which was famous for its majestic triple-towered cathedral and medieval buildings. Here, parades and training took place on the town's racecourse. However, within a short period, the Battalion was on the move again. Even at this point in the war, fears of a German invasion prevailed and on 30th April, the unit transferred to Mablethorpe to form part of the Lincolnshire Coastal Defence. Now renamed the 5th (Reserve) North Staffords, they were camped in a large field near the railway station, but also occupied several buildings in the resort as offices and stores. Trenches and machine gun emplacements were constructed along the shoreline and at night barbed wire was thrown across the High Street. Concrete pill boxes on the sand dunes were manned daily for 24hrs, and from dusk until dawn the sands were patrolled to give warnings of any impending attack. In the holiday months the patrols were said to have had a busy time in *'driving back not Germans, but visitors who sought the solitude of the sand hills in the evening!'* However, a most popular event during the summer months for the troops was when they marched to the beach for a morning dip. Colonel Blizzard was also a regular sight in the town as he visited the various companies on his huge white horse 'Snowdrop'. Not perhaps surprisingly at this period, the resort proved to be popular with some North Staffordshire folk who took the opportunity to visit serving relatives and friends before they were drafted overseas and the town was said, at times, to be a veritable *'Stoke-on-Sea!'* [5]

In addition to coastal defence obligations, the Battalion was a 'feeder unit' replacing front-line casualties for the $2^{nd}/5^{th}$ and $2^{nd}/6^{th}$ North Staffords who were serving with the 59th Division. Consequently, the progress of the war and the fortunes of the allies could, at times, be judged by the frequency and size of the drafts of men despatched to fill the gaps in France and on occasions when troops were leaving, Colonel Blizzard was on the railway station platform to shake hands with every departing soldier as they boarded the troop train for Folkestone.[6] The Reserve Battalion was also responsible for wounded or sick men from the North Staffords who had returned from France, and the resort and unit was said to provide a *'happy time'* given the circumstances. Unfortunately for Charles Masefield, it was to be his fate to exchange this peaceful environment for the grim realities of battle and daily hardship conditions of the Western Front.

Notes

1   *Staffordshire Sentinel.* 6 Jan 1917.
2   *Ibid*, 11 Jan 1917.
3   F. J. Johnson, *op.cit,* p. 21 & p. 181.
4   Lt Walter Meakin, *op.cit,* p. 85.
5   *Ibid*, p. 98.
6   Gilbert Wright, 'Mablethorpe 1916' in *Lincolnshire Life* May 1983.

*A Postcard of Brocton Camp taken during the First World War
(Photo from Author's Collection)*

*Preparing Food at a Field Kitchen, Brocton Camp during World War I
(Photo from the Staffordshire Archives)*

Contemporary Lincoln when Charles' Regiment was stationed there
Early 20th Century Postcards of Lincoln
(Postcards from Author's Collection)

11

ATTACK AT DAWN!

On 5th May 1917 Charles Masefield embarked for France where he rejoined his regiment which by this time was in operations at Lens. Writing to his wife on 27th May from his cellar billet during a brief respite from action, he provides details of the war damage locally while coincidentally managing somehow to maintain a sense of humour. He explains that the postman on his rounds would *'hardly recognise the houses on his usual beat.'* The properties opposite were *'in ruins - heaps of bricks scattered about or barbed wire across them.'* Some gave the impression of being hastily abandoned. Then, somewhat tongue in cheek, he continues that *'something ought to be done about the objects of metal which are constantly falling about the neighbourhood making an intolerable din. There'll be some nasty accidents with them before long, I'm certain if people aren't more careful. Some of these things are of a kind I haven't had thrown at me before and I'm not much attracted to them.*

There are some called Flying Prawns which are as good as a firework display at night as they look like shooting stars of the finest variety. But your interest in them is rather marred by your anxiety as to where they're coming down. Though they are amiable trifles compared with the heavy trench mortars which we all have the strongest objection to, if they come anywhere in your neighbourhood the concussion fairly leaves you gasping as you are not sure whether you're still in one piece or not!'

Not having received a letter from Muriel recently, Charles wrote that he was *'hoping for a splendid rush of arrears of correspondence'* and enquires if she had ordered a newspaper for him - *'I haven't seen one for 3 or 4 days.'* The letter concludes with a limerick which he had been inspired to compose by his accommodation -

'There was an old man in a cellar,
A queer, unaccountable feller,
For he wanted his wife
Though the shells were so rife,
So he wrote to that lady to tell her!'

Meanwhile, the sartorial **BEF Times** was

continuing to bring light relief to those involved in the grim situation on the Western Front. The edition of 10th April 1917 features correspondence purporting to be from *'a peaceful citizen'* objecting to *'the planting of a 12ins howitzer in the middle of his smallholding.'* *'Fed up'* writes that although he is admittedly *'somewhat behind with his rates, the injustice of the present conditions is apparent.'* He concludes that if nothing is done on the matter, he will vote against the present candidate at the forthcoming elections! That same edition also contains a fabricated advertisement on behalf of a company whose hotels are *'pleasantly and airily situated in pretty parts of France with excellent views FACING THE FRONT.'* Further information reveals *'good shooting in the area'* and that the proprietors strongly recommend any of the hotels *'to all gentlemen (?) of GERMAN NATIONALITY who are in need of a real rest after the noise and nerve strain on life in the trenches.'*

On 24th May Charles Masefield was gazetted Acting Captain (A/Capt) and put in charge of a Company *'very pleasing for me'* he wrote to a relative on 3rd June. The correspondence is addressed from *'a cellar in France (lately the residence of Herr Von - !)'* His accommodation is described as being *'under a ruined house with several feet of concrete erected on top of it...so we're able to defy anything short of a direct hit from a really heavy shell.'* As a result, Charles admits to feeling *'quite an affection for the Boche who designed the commodious dwelling. He's been at great pains to make it shell proof'.* However, whilst this was the case, Charles confessed to being *'a bit bored with cellars when the weather is as lovely as it has been'.* In a more serious vein, he continued that *'tonight we go up into the line again...we get shelled - trench mortared rather unpleasantly at times but otherwise its not such a bad spot.'* He also mentions that *'one of our patrols met a couple of the enemy the other night and killed them both.'*

In the meantime, the recent Battle of Arras had given the British possession of Vimy Ridge to the east as far as Lens, but the escarpment then continued north in the direction of Ypres. Known as the Messines Ridge, this was to be the next objective. The assault by British and Anzac troops was launched on 7th June, prefaced by the detonation of 21 enormous mines, the effect of which was felt as an earthquake in England! The offensive was one of the most successful allied efforts, aided by the use of a highly effective creeping artillery barrage. Counter attacks by the Germans failed and the whole of the ridge including Hill 60 near Ypres was captured. Over 7,000 prisoners were taken and a vast amount of guns and equipment was seized.

The 5th North Staffords continued in operations in and around Lens and were involved in much of the fighting in areas of the town known as Cités. This proved very difficult as the trenches ran amongst ruined streets and houses. In retreating, the Germans had begun to burn and destroy as much as they could, and there were dense columns of dark smoke everywhere. On 11th June, Charles wrote of the fighting in the *'streets of ruined houses - miles of them almost everyone with gaping holes in walls or roofs.'* Patrolling at night was *'nervy work'* he explained, as there were so many possible places where snipers could conceal themselves. This was in complete contrast to the *'fairly lazy time'* they had when behind the line. *'The trouble is'* he disclosed, *'we never go back far enough to get a decent bath or change. It's weeks since I took my clothes off at night and the weather has been hot'* since his arrival.

On 14th June, the 5th North Staffords were involved in a planned raid at Cité St. Laurent. According to the official regimental history, the operation was carried out by two groups chosen from 'A' and 'C' Companies, comprising 8 officers and 160 men. Having been withdrawn for prior training, they were then moved into the line on 13th June. On the following day, the raid was preceded by a bombardment, the two groups then advancing across No Man's Land. 'A' Company on the right was commanded by Capt. Benjamin Harold Rayner, whilst on the left 'C' Company was led by A/Capt Charles Masefield. On reaching the enemy wire, 'A' Company was heavily bombarded and driven back. In attempting another attack, Capt. Rayner was killed and the Company had to return without entering the enemy trenches. However, 'C' Company was successful in making gaps in the enemy wire, resulting in two men subsequently being awarded the Military Medal. A first wave under Lt. Basil Green then put out a covering party, making their way into the dugouts and cellars and inflicted heavy casualties.

The second wave under Masefield then cleared the trenches and dugouts involving *'a considerable amount of fighting,'* he personally killing two of the enemy at close quarters before successfully withdrawing his men. It was later learned that in the operation, the Battalion had lost 3 officers, 13 men were killed or missing and 37 wounded. For their gallantry on the raid, it was subsequently announced that Charles and fellow officer Basil Green were to be awarded the Military Cross. [1]

The citation in respect of Charles' award reads as follows: *'For conspicuous gallantry and devotion to duty. During a raid upon enemy trenches, he led his company with great dash and skill under heavy trench mortar barrage, attacking a party of the enemy single-handed and killing two at close quarters. At least 50 of the enemy were killed and 3 prisoners taken, after which he withdrew his company, having shown conspicuous gallantry and good leadership throughout.'* [2]

Regardless of the war situation that he found himself in, Charles maintained regular correspondence with his beloved Muriel, writing lengthy letters including news from the Front. No particular reference is made in his letter of 19th June 1917 of the action of a few days earlier, other than having been pulled out of the line for two days to prepare for the raid. However, he did refer to Lt. Herbert Evans Smith who had only been with him '*a few days*' and was '*as keen as mustard.*' It was considered that the officer would have been '*a great acquisition*' but unfortunately he was killed in action during the raid. Charles wrote that he had ridden over to his funeral, having '*sent a firing party to fire over the grave and buglers to blow the Last Post.*' It was '*a terribly moving night and sound.*' In a lighter vein, reference was made to the weather, '*the heat having abated at last, thank goodness. It broke in thunderstorms yesterday and the temperature is perfect today. Till yesterday we had been existing on slices of lemon in water and lettuces and cherries. We've scoured the neighbourhood for cucumbers with no result*' and requested '*a parcel of two or three now and again - they would be most thankfully received.*' Revealing that he and his colleagues were '*having an excellent rest with parades in the mornings and afternoons generally free.*' He was enjoying rides on a horse called 'Tommy' - '*he's rather lazy going out, but comes home at a great pace.'* Concluding the correspondence, Charles describes the area of the war zone in which he is based - *'a model village with all the houses in twos, detached from any others and surrounded by gardens which are full of fruit and vegetables. I doubt if there is anything like it in England. It belongs to the Colliery Co. The pit, by the way, is only worked at night now as the smoke from it would certainly draw Boche shells. The people are very friendly too. We sheltered from a storm this morning in a cottage and the old dame regaled us with black coffee - very good!'*

However Charles did choose to comment on the recent action two days later when on 21st June he wrote to a relative - *'looking back on it, it was of course a bloody and beastly business but at the time one was quite drunken with victory and the elemental instinct of kill that you be not killed, and it is only through killing that the whole horrible job will some day or other be ended.'*

Writing a brief letter to Muriel on 26th June, Charles commented that they had moved *'up again last night, but are not quite in the line yet'*. Again, he touched on the devastation around him and the *'streets of smashed* houses' with *'lots of furniture, all an inch deep in mortar dust.'* He expressed his surprise having seen some of the things that had survived - *'a billiard table in its old place for instance. We picked up some crockery which will come in useful for our mess.'*

It was to be only a short period before the 5th North Staffords were to be involved in action again. On this occasion the objective was the capture of Lens itself, the town being a formidable position. Having taken many prisoners, it was learned that the German forces in that area of the line were becoming demoralised. As a consequence, the High Command considered that there was a possibility of capturing the town before the worn out German Division was relieved and replaced with fresh troops. This conclusion having been reached, it was decided to mount the attack on the morning of Sunday 1st July.

According to the official regimental history, 3 Brigades of the 46th Division were to launch the attack from the Souchez River in the south - 139th (Sherwoods) Brigade on the left; the 137th (Staffords) in the centre, with the 138th (Lincolns & Leicesters) on the right. In relation to the 137th Brigade, the 5th North Staffords were detailed to lead the attack with the 6th South Staffords to the rear supplying 'mopping up' parties and local reserves. All the Battalions were described as being '*very weak in numbers*' due to the constant fighting. Also, the strength of the Companies was '*so small*' that it was decided to have only 2 platoons per Company. The assault was then to be made on a 4 Company front, each attacking in two waves. The two waves assembled in two rows of trenches at 2.00 a.m., the prime objective being the Cité du Moulin, originally the western suburb of Lens. Each man of the 5th North Staffords was issued with 150 rounds of ammunition, 2 bombs, and 2 days rations. In attacking, 'B' Company was to the left (2/Lt A. W. Boulton in command), then 'A' Company (2/Lt P. B. Ross); 'C' Company (A/Capt C. Masefield) with 'D' Company (A/Capt A. T. Scrivener) on the extreme right.

The attack area consisted of four streets with houses on both sides, the two central thoroughfares leading into a small square with a church. While some of the houses were in a state of semi-collapse with only portions of walls remaining, others were almost intact.

The German first trench lay inside the town, its wires having already been cut in preparation for the attack, and repairs had been prevented by firing shrapnel. A creeping barrage was to assist the attack which was to commence at 2.43a.m, just before dawn.

At first the advance progressed favourably with the men passing through the area of cut wire into the streets. 'A' and 'B' Companies then met resistance from German machine guns and failed to reach their objective. Meeting less opposition, 'C' and 'D' Companies advanced down the streets reaching the so called 'Aconite' trench, leaving the 6th South Staffords in 'mopping up' operations. 'C' and 'D' Companies then worked their way to the left, the intention being to meet up with 'A' Company. Unfortunately, the Sherwoods on the left, despite their efforts, had also failed to reach their objective as did the Lincolns and Leicesters to the right. The sad result was, that although 'C' and 'D' Companies had succeeded in reaching their objective and consolidated their positions, they were cut off from supporting troops. The remainder of the 5th North Staffords under Major F.C. Wenger made unavailing attempts to reach their stricken colleagues, meeting severe hand to hand fighting. Eventually, Major Wenger himself was wounded in a German counterattack. Reinforcements from the 6th North Staffords also failed to get through, suffering heavy casualties. Finally, at 7.00 a.m, the attempt to rescue the two stranded Companies was abandoned. Total casualties of the 46th Division amounted to 50 officers and 1,000 men. The attack had been a failure, the Germans possibly having brought in a fresh Division. [3]

At this stage, the fate of 'C' and 'D' Companies was uncertain, and A/Captain Charles Masefield and others were reported as missing.

Notes

1 Lt. W. Meakin, *op.cit,* pp. 89 - 90.
2 *London Gazette.* 24 Aug 1917. Surprisingly, the relevant entry incorrectly describes Charles Masefield's rank as 2/Lt at the time, when he was a Captain!
3 Lt. W. Meakin, *op.cit,* pp. 91 - 93.

*Map from the History of the 5th North Staffords 1914 – 1919
by Lt. Walter Meakin
(Hughes & Harber Ltd, Longton, 1920)*

Ruins of the Museum and Cathedral at Arras following War Damage
(Postcard from Author's Collection)

Ruins of the Principal Square in Lens following War Damage
(Postcard from Author's Collection)

12

A PERIOD OF UNCERTAINTY

Unlike with today's advancement of modern communication including the epidemic of mobile telephones, one can assume the first indication of grim news from the Front was that of a telegram delivered by the Post Office Telegram Boy as he went about his duties on a bicycle. In the case of Charles Masefield, the dreaded knock on the door occurred on 8th July 1917 when the following telegram was received by his wife at 'Hanger Hill' from the Officer i/c Territorial Force Records, Lichfield -

'Regret to inform you 2/Lt C. J. B. Masefield, 5th North Staffs Regt is reported missing...this does not necessarily mean that he is killed. Further information will be notified you immediately same is received.'

Thus followed a period of agonising uncertainty for the Masefield family, whilst at the same time a flame of hope burned that Charles may still be alive. What the family did not know at this stage was that during the attack on Lens, Charles had been mortally wounded and captured by the Germans in that condition. Then, on 24th August, followed publication in the **London Gazette** of the official announcement of the award of the Military Cross to Charles for *'conspicuous gallantry and devotion to duty'* during the earlier action of 14th June. Sadly, the announcement came too late for him to know of it. The first official notification of Charles' death was received by Muriel Masefield on 28th September 1917. This was by way of a telegram from Buckingham Palace expressing the deep regret of the King and Queen *'at the loss you and the army have sustained by the death of your husband in the service of his country. Their Majesties truly sympathise with you in your sorrow.'* A memorial service was subsequently held in the Parish Church at Cheadle which included *'a most inspiring sermon'* preached by Rev. G. W. Philips, Rector of Cheadle, a personal friend of the family.

Nevertheless, it was not until 2nd October that an official Death Certificate was issued by the War Office. This resulted from the receipt of a report from the German Government through the Red Cross confirming that 2/Lt.

Charles John Beech Masefield had died at Leforest on 2nd July 1917. An accompanying letter, however, stated that *'no report of the burial of the officer has been received.'* As it happened, it was to be another distressing 3 months before Muriel Masefield received confirmation of the interment of her beloved husband's remains. The War Office had immediately queried the question of burial following notification of Charles' death, but it was not until 18th January 1918 that confirmation was received that his remains had, in fact, been buried with full military honours in Grave No.117 in the Parish Cemetery at Leforest. The official document also discloses that Lt. Masefield was *'brought into the Lazaret* (i.e. military hospital or field hospital) *shot in the abdomen on 1st July 1917 and died on 2nd July 1917 without gaining consciousness. His personal belongings have been sent through diplomatic channels to be delivered to the next of kin.'* [1]

Surviving hitherto unpublished documents provide a few details of what transpired during that final part of the failed action at Lens which led to the capture and subsequent death of Charles Masefield. These should not be dismissed simply on the ground that they are not 'official', as they were written by men who were there. Their views may differ in some respects to those recorded 'officially' but as the author of the regimental history admits *'there are some inconsistencies between accounts, but this is always the case in a battle.'* [2] It is inevitable that there will be some confusion and this comment is supported by 2/Lt. R. F. Johnson who later wrote that in the heat of the action *'bullets were flying like sand on a desert on a windy day!'* [3] A note written on 15th July by No.202453 Pte. James Bennett Shenton confirms that 'C' and 'D' Companies were cut off and that Major C.E. Graham died leading 'A' and 'B' Companies in their unsuccessful rescue attempt. A member of the Signalling Section, Bennett Shenton also wrote that *'nothing will shake my belief that your husband* (i.e Charles Masefield) *is a prisoner of war - for I do know that he was not wounded from the time he left our lines up to reaching the houses in which were the Boches.'* On the other hand, 2/Lt. R. F. Johnson believed that Charles Masefield's wound was *'not very serious, a bullet in the right thigh, but he had lost a lot of blood.'* He also suggests that Charles may have been *'caught by our own barrage which was put up in answer to our SOS signal.'* No.201835 Pte. James Rose was another surviving member of the 5th North Staffords. Writing after the war, he described being captured at Lens and that he was taken to some barbed wire *'where we saw Lt. Masefield who was wounded in the upper thigh.'* He was initially carried to a dressing station and then transferred by motor ambulance to a hospital *'some distance behind the line.'* The letter also states that *'we left Lt. Masefield in fair condition.'* [4]

Many tributes were paid to Charles Masefield, not only from fellow officers and men, but from various organisations with which he had been associated before military service. Charles no doubt could not have wished for a finer epitaph than the tribute contained in a letter from a brother officer which reads, *'We are all awfully proud of him; he played such a valiant part and thoroughly deserved his MC.'* Or the remark to his sister of one of his men: *'He was a real gentleman. I would have followed him anywhere.'* [5] Bennett Shenton also wrote that, *'Nobody had a better name than Mr. Masefield, he would do anything for his men and they for him.'* Brother officer 2/Lt. R. F. Johnson in correspondence referred to the death at Lens of 2/Lt. J. E. Lowe who had earlier been awarded the Military Cross for a night raid on German trenches on 19th September 1916 and commented, *'had Scrivener's and Masefield's behaviour that night come to light, they would have been similarly decorated, as they deserved them, as they both had a splendid record of work in the 1/5th North Staffs.'* Like Charles, fellow officer Alwynne Twyford Scrivener held the rank of A/Captain and he also died of wounds at Lens. Colonel A. E. Blizzard, Commanding Officer of the 5th Territorial Force (R) Battalion, North Staffs Regiment subsequently wrote of Charles that *'he, like many others, knew nothing of military life until the outbreak of war, but as soon as circumstances permitted placed his services at the disposal of his King and country. Into his new profession as a soldier, in his quiet dignified way, he threw all his talents and enthusiasm, became a most competent officer always to be relied upon, and commanded the love and admiration of his brother officers and the NCOs and men who served with him.*

When the supreme test came he gallantly led a gallant band in the assault, and held on to the position gained, where unfortunately supports could not reach them, and where he lost his life, all those who were not killed being captured. The Regiment mourns the loss of a good man and gallant officer, whose services added lustre to the splendid traditions created by those who had gone before. He has left a memory which will be cherished by all those who knew him, and I feel the loss of a true friend.' [6]

The North Staffs Miners' High Education Movement was an organisation of which Charles had founded the Cheadle Branch, and, in doing so, had established a series of regular lectures. Following the AGM in July 1918, its Joint Hon. Secretary wrote to John Masefield, Charles' father, expressing sincere and respectful sympathy to all members of the family '*in the heavy bereavement sustained. Charles Masefield took a very real interest in the movement and gave it unstinted encouragement and practical help...his influence and memory will be in the truest sense an inspiration to us all.*' [7] Likewise, the North Staffs Field Club published a lengthy '*In Memoriam*' in its Transations (Vol. L11

1917-18) and announced the posthumous award of the Garner Medal in recognition of Charles' excellent services to the organisation.

Of Charles and his work, Arthur St. John Adcock wrote *'that he was still only finding himself as a poet is apparent to anyone who reads what he has written. His philosophy of life is clear and consistent throughout, but a comparison of his last with his earlier poems reveals a sure, continuous maturing in thought and expression and a still-growing mastery of his art. There is much of authentic achievement in his work, but even more of promise, that can never now be fulfilled.'* He also added that *'we should remember...that he and his comrades did not die for the old England, but for a new England of their dreams that we shall realise if we are as loyal to them as they were to us.'* [8]

Charles' friend, C.H. Poole described him as *'a lovable and gentle character, energetic and sincere...In the war he fought bravely for his ideals and, although hating war, joined in its conflicts, believing that 'Right is Might' and that good should eventually overcome evil for,'* to quote Charles' own words from his poem **Going** *out to Victory –*

'We are chosen; we are sealed;
Unto us is Truth revealed,
Great may the foe be, but we are the greater,
Often, no doubt, we shall falter and fail,
Crushed by his power - but soon or later
Right is Might, and we shall prevail'.[9]

Charles' last poem was composed in May 1917, shortly before his death. In this, it may be seen that he seemed calmly to accept as inevitable the imminence of his death and that his grave would be in foreign soil -

'In Honorem Fortium
I sometimes think that I have lived too long,
Who have heard so many a gay brave singer's song
Fail him for ever - seen so many sails
Lean out resplendent to the evil gales,
Then Death, the wrecker, get his harvest in.
Oh, ill it is, when men lose all, to win;

Grief though it be to die, 'tis grief yet more
To live and count the dear dead comrades o'er.
Peace. After all you died not. We've no fear
But that, long ages hence, you will be near -
A thought by night - on the warm wind a breath,
Making for courage, putting by old Death,
Living wherever men are not afraid
Of aught but making bravery a parade.
Yes, parleying with fear, they'll pause and say
'At Gommecourt boys suffered worse that day;'
Or, hesitating on some anxious brink,
They will become heroic when they think
'Did they not rise mortality above
Who staked a lifetime all made sweet with love?'

Notes

1. Berlin SW11. Ab.V. Griessineger to the International Committee of the Red Cross 5 Dec 1917.
2. Lt. W. Meakin, *op.cit*, p. 96.
3. Letter to his father written whilst interned as a POW at Frieburg; an extract of which was forwarded was forwarded to Charles' father by Mr R. Moore on 23 Oct 1917.
4. Letter to father of Lt. J. W. Greeves dated 3 Jan 1919. Greeves was also killed in action at Lens on 1 July 1917.
5. Quoted by A. St. John Adcock in foreword to C. J. B. Masefield *Poems* (Oxford: Blackwell, 1919) p. 7.
6. *Ibid*, p. 8. It is interesting to note that Colonel Blizzard married Charles' sister Margaret in 1937, following which they lived at 'Hill Crest.'
7. Letter to Charles' father 24 July 1918.
8. A. St. John Adcock, *op.cit*, pp. 6 - 7.
9. *Poets of the Shires - Staffordshire* (N. Ling & Co, 1928) p. 275.

Charles Masefield's Grave at Leforest
(Photo Courtesy of Robin Masefield)

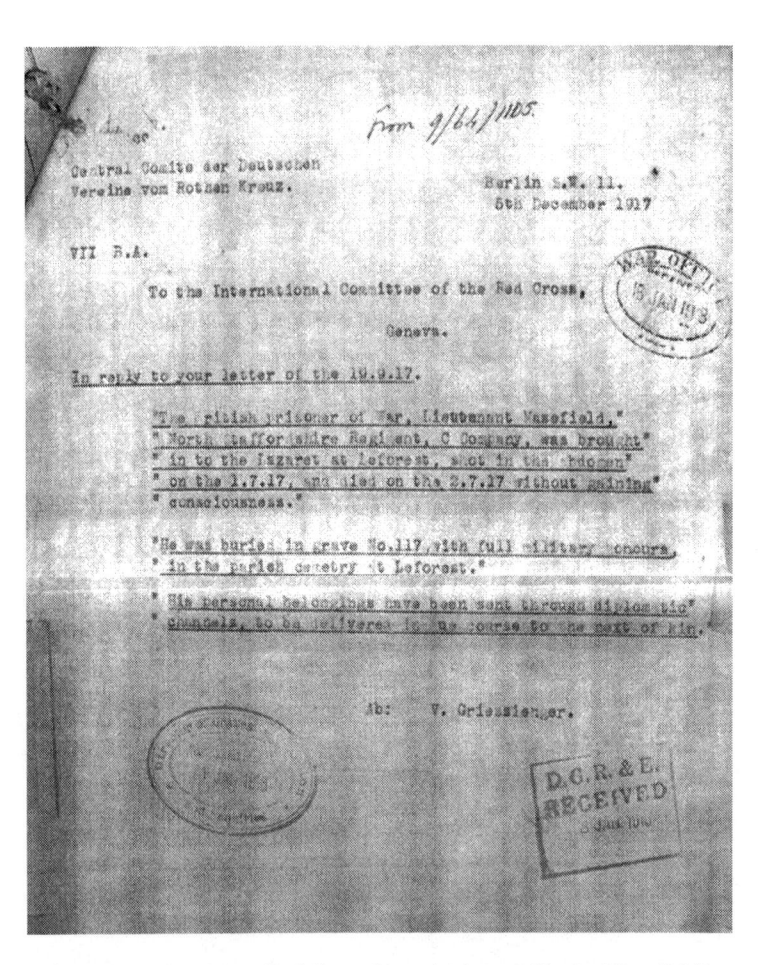

*German Notification to Red Cross Organisation of Charles Masefield's
Death and Burial at Leforest
(Taken from Author's Collection)*

13

LETTERS OF FAREWELL

Throughout history, soldiers have appreciated that they run a high risk of being killed in the service of their country, and they have written farewell letters to loved ones in the event of their death. These attempt to impart their final thoughts, perhaps on the eve of a battle, or sometimes as they lay mortally wounded in the field. These items of personal correspondence provide a final enduring link with the writer, and a haunting voice from beyond the grave. Yet having written such letters some, of course, were fortunate to survive and went on to fight another day.

Charles Masefield was no exception in having written farewell letters. As might be expected, these were written to his wife and son at Rouen on 21st June 1916 prior to being moved up into the fighting line. Having said that, Charles was fortunate to survive in the war for another year. The letter to his wife reads as follows:

'My own darling, darling wife,

Goodbye. When you read this you will have heard that I have met my death and I hope I shall have met it without flinching.

I have written a longish letter to Geoff (sweet little soul!) because I wanted to say some things to him which he isn't old enough yet to understand, but I needn't say much to you, my darling. Only I entirely believe that we are separated for a little while only, and if it is permitted me to help or strengthen you in spirit while you are still on earth, you know that I shall always be very near you at your need.

You have made the last years of my life a dream of happiness, my sweet. You have loved me with a love so unshakeable and so abundant that it has sometimes made me ashamed, because I felt I was not worthy of it. And when we had to make the great decision about my joining the army you upheld me with such sureness and such courage, though you knew that if I fell yours would be infinitely the harder lot.

You will be one now of that proud great army of women who, having given their all ungrudgingly to help *save the world, have won the right to the gratitude of generations unborn.*

You will (thank God) have Geoff to live for, and no mother could wish for a finer little son. May he ever be a joy to you, and may God in his goodness comfort and strengthen you both until we meet again.
Your ever loving husband,
Charlie'.

The lengthy letter addressed to his son, referred to in the above correspondence to Muriel reads as follows:
'My darling Geoff,
I am expecting very soon to be in the fighting line, bearing my part as well as I can in the finest cause man ever fought for - the cause of the world's freedom and peace and human brotherhood. And as of course I have to recognise that I may be killed, I want to write down a few things which you will be able to read when you are old enough.

Never grieve for me if I should die. I have had a very happy life mostly, and in my marriage to your darling mother I have been unspeakably happy always - and you have been a pure delight and joy to us. I can't think that Death will really separate me from you both. The object of life is not to eke it out to the last dregs, but to use it to the best purpose, and no one could use life better than by giving it gladly and ungrudgingly in this war. So if I die, the sorrow will not be mine, but your mother's and yours, because I shan't be able to help you in the years to come. You will just have to help each other as best you can. I don't want to fetter either of you with schemes and directions, because I can't tell how circumstances will change around you, but I think there is just one thing I can do for you, and that is to write down here a few things to help you to get at the principles we all have to get at to build our lives on.

First of all, try to be a Christian. We can none of us succeed but don't let that discourage you. Endeavour is our meat and drink - the very diet of our nature. Success is a heady, flat, unsatisfying draught. So go on trying and failing, trying and failing always. And don't be content with the externals and ecclesiastical traditions. Go to the inmost core - the spirit of Christ himself, and try as you live longer to get nearer to understanding it. It is really all of Christianity that matters. Don't accept it at second-hand, as you value your own soul. If I had to put my own religion in a phrase, I think I should define it as a passionate belief in the Fatherhood of God and the brotherhood of man. But the older I grow, the less I like priests and parsons and churches and sects (and it seems to me Christ didn't like them either).

As to men and women, take them as you find them, and make the best of them. I am always changing my opinions as to the good and the bad amongst us, and the least likeable have often shamed me by their loveableness. And remember that there are two classes of vices. Some are human and warm, and some inhuman and cold. By the last I mean such things as hypocrisy, meanness, spite, and such reptile births, sprung of an innate repulsion from the live, generous and open spirit. Have no truck with men and women who are capable of things like these. But at the other end of the scale are the vices which are vices, it is true, yet they imply no disease of the spirit, but only a superabundance of warm blood -virtue carried to excess. So I say choose for your friends happy, warm-hearted men and women, and as long as you remember your honour you will not go far wrong.

As to politics, I can't tell whether you will have any leanings towards that. In England it has for some time now been a rather dirty game, and in other countries it is perhaps dirtier. No doubt democracy is the only possible form of government in a civilised state, but it ought not to mean a truckling of the leaders to the people. Leaders must lead, not follow, guide, not merely rush, shouting down the popular road. They must win men's votes by convincing them, not cheat them out of them by currying favour with them. I would sooner not engage in politics at all than engage in it on any terms but these. And Party Government, inevitable as it may be, is a vile thing if it blinds a man to his own side's faults and the other side's virtues. Scheming, wire pulling, place-hunting are among the things which the politician finds himself sliding into imperceptibly if he is not very wary of demeaning himself. Yet I believe a clean man might do much to rescue politics from its dirt.

You will come, as you grow older, into the midst of many temptations. But you will have many things to help you - your horror of doing anything which would make your mother ashamed of you, and your knowledge that you are a man of honour and a gentleman. Your honour is "the white bird within your breast" that must always be kept unsullied, and must always be obeyed, no matter what the cost.

Whatever profession you adopt, work hard at it, not for the sake of the money you will get by it, but for the sake of doing the work well. Work hard until you come to have an instinctive repulsion from scamping a piece of work. And you will have your reward, for it is work that makes people happy, lack of it that makes them a nuisance to themselves and to others.

You will be happy, I think, if you will frame your life on the plans I have set out for you here as well as I can. They are the plans I have tried to frame mine on, from the age when I was old enough to work them out for myself. And perhaps you may be helped by having them before you are old enough to discover all of them unaided.

Don't be afraid of being happy. Life is very sweet and very dreadful. You must accept the dreadfulness; accept with open hands the sweetness, the dear human relations, the sheer rollicking fun of life, the calm healing loveliness of nature, too.

And if ever you feel weak, think how many weak men have done strong and splendid things. Learn to love the stories of great and noble deeds - of King David pouring out the water which had imperilled men's lives, of Garibaldi who his passion for Italy nerving him to the deeds of a demi-god, of Captain Oates walking out into the snow to try to save his comrades.
Good-bye, my dear, dear son -
Your ever loving
Father.'

Somehow in between preparations for the attack of 1st July, Charles managed to write one final letter to Muriel. Briefly headed *'BEF'* and dated 30th June 1917 it reads as follows:

'My own,
We attack the Boche in the small hours of tomorrow morning, so by the time you get this it will all have been well over for some time, and if you have had no wire you will know that all is well with me. Moreover, within 24 hours of the attack we are being relieved and going back for a real rest.

Well, three things may happen. If I come through all right I shall have helped to give the enemy another good knock, and I shall be very proud of it again! If I get a good Blighty, by the time you get this I shall be in England. And if the third thing happens at any rate I have pulled off the raid the other day all right and so not soldiered in vain, and I know you won't sorrow only, but be very proud that you and I have offered up the greatest sacrifice we could offer for the finest cause of our time.

I am very busy of course with arrangements and organization, and haven't time to write much and if we take the Boche positions I don't know if I shall be able to send back a field postcard tomorrow. But if you don't hear you will know all is well.

Oh my darling, my darling loved! It's a beastly wet day which makes things rather unpleasant, but it's as bad for the Boche of course. But there's plenty of time yet for the weather to clear before we move up to the line to 'go over'.

A thousand kisses for that ancient (i.e Geoff).

Yours as ever,

Charlie'.

Nearly a century later, Charles Masefield's letters carry great resonance. They are a surviving memorial and a voice that still speaks clearly from the grave and loudly on behalf of the writer. As one former teacher once observed - *'In pain of death, spoken words often fail, but words written down last forever.'*

14

VICTORY ACHIEVED... ANOTHER BATTLE BEGINS!

At the beginning of 1918 it seemed highly unlikely that a victory would be achieved during that year, and plans were being drawn up by allied commanders for 1919 and even beyond. In particular, the Americans were of the opinion that the war would not be over quickly, and General John Joseph Pershing was anticipating having 100 divisions in France before hostilities finally ceased. In turn, Germany appreciated that if it had any chance of winning the war, it would have to be before the Americans gained more experience of the type of warfare being fought on the Western Front. Also, at this time, Germany was aware that the British and French forces were recovering from operations of the previous year. Meanwhile, in Russia, the Tsar's regime had been overthrown and the new Bolshevik government sued for peace with Germany, culminating with the signing of a peace treaty on 3rd March ending hostilities on the Eastern

Front. This resulted in the release of German troops from that area of warfare, enabling them to be transferred to the Western Front.

As a consequence, on 21st March, a year after abandoning their trenches on the Somme for the greater safety of the Hindenburg line, the Germans launched a new offensive, the intention being to force a wedge between the British and French forces. Said to be largely the brainchild of General Erich Von Ludendorff, Operation 'Michael' was aimed at British positions at Arras. Aided by the cover of thick mist, German troops swiftly advanced, causing havoc along the British front line. Its initial success was enormous with the speed of penetration so fast that many of the British rear gun batteries were overwhelmed before they could commence firing. Within a few days the allied lines were broken and by 5th April the British were defending a line 10 miles west of Amiens, and the whole of the Somme region so hard won in 1916 was now back in German hands. But having made an orderly retreat and now reinforced by French reservists, the British line held firm. The Germans then halted their offensive on the Somme and transferred their attention to Flanders. On 9th April they attacked the Ypres salient aiming to seize the railway junction at Hazebrouck opening up the road to the Channel ports. They were brought to a halt some 5 miles west of the town, and the gravity of the situation was reflected in Commander-in-Chief Haig's now famous *'Backs to the wall'* order of the day for 11th April - *'Every position must be held to the last man...each one must fight on to the end. The safety of our homes and freedom of mankind alike depend upon the conduct of each one of us at this critical moment.'*

On 24th April for the first time in the war, British and German tanks met in combat at Cachy, resulting in a successful engagement for the allies. This was followed up by the recapture of the village of Villers-Bretonneux by British and Australian troops. On 29th April Ludendorff called off the offensive, his troops now exhausted and hungry. Also, where the British had retreated, supplies of food had been sabotaged to prevent them falling into enemy hands. However, not all had been completely destroyed and German soldiers had been astonished on finding the quality and quantity of foodstuffs available to the British troops. It is believed that this helped to undermine morale in the German troops. [1] In addition, there was increasing civil unrest in Germany with the army's needs receiving priority. In complete contrast, Britain had taken measures to ensure that, as far as possible, the civilian population was 'taken care of.' This resulted from a propaganda campaign encouraging a 'we're in this together' and the imposition of rationing. The Germans had not adopted this approach.

The next German offensive came on 27th May with amazing results, they succeeding in managing to advance 10 miles in a single day. Fourteen divisions broke through on a 24 mile front in the French sector between Soissons and Rhiems. As it happened, four battle-fatigued British divisions had been sent to the area for a rest only to find themselves in the path of the German advance. By 3rd June German troops were within 40 miles of Paris. Localised fighting continued throughout that month with the Germans attempting to extend their gains, and on 15th July Ludendorff launched a further offensive on a 50 mile front of the Marne. They succeeded in crossing the river but were held by American troops, and the ensuing battle saw the French recapture Soissons.

On 8th August it was the turn of the British to launch an offensive with over 400 tanks advancing across the Somme battlefields. Aided by a thick mist they succeeded in advancing 6 miles, the encounter becoming known as the Battle of Amiens. A war correspondent who witnessed the event wrote that it was *'one of the greatest single feats of arms in the annals of the British Army, and the arms were of the strangest and most various sorts. On the ground were our iron horses on caterpillar feet; 300ft above flew airmen whose impudent audacity has never been excelled.'* (2) The action appeared to have a significant form of psychological effect on the Germans who up to this point had been striving for victory on the Western Front. But also, the number of prisoners being taken was testament to the enemy's rapidly eroding will to resist, having poorer quality worn out equipment.

With increasing momentum the allies began to drive the Germans back, advancing on all fronts. On 4th

October the *Sentinel* reported that the British had crossed the Hindenburg Line, finally reaching open countryside after four long years of trench warfare. On the following day the newspaper announced that German troops were abandoning their positions on the Flanders coast and that Prince Max of Baden had sent a note to America's President Woodrow Wilson, on behalf of the German Government, requesting him to *'take up the question of bringing about peace.'* Ludendorff's resignation followed on 25th October, he being replaced by General Groener. Having a more realistic idea of the way that the war was going, Groener immediately began seeking an armistice with the allies. Also, recognising that there was likely to be a revolution if he remained in power, Kaiser Wilhelm II abdicated on 9th November and accepted an offer from the Dutch to take up exile in Holland. With the abdication, the last barrier to peace had gone and an armistice was swiftly agreed. On 9th November the *Sentinel* announced that newly appointed German Chancellor Friedrich Ebert had accepted the armistice terms offered by French Marshall Foche on behalf of the victorious allies, and at 11am on 11th

November the guns fell silent. The terrible carnage was finally over.

In London guns boomed forth and church bells rang out as official signs that the war was over. These were joined by the people's contributions to the sounds of victory including klaxon horns on vehicles, whistles, bugles and almost anything else, be it instrumental or otherwise, which would make a noise. **The Times** and other newspapers reported *'cheering crowds'* and *'rejoicing in the streets'* and this was repeated throughout Britain with colliery and factory hooters joining in the cacophony of noise in the industrial areas.

At the time, no one really appreciated how great the casualties had been, but it was subsequently learned that in France and Belgium alone, more than ¾ million had died. Twenty thousand had died on the Somme, to be later regarded as an utterly pointless slaughter and retained in the national memory as a major indictment of those generals concerned. The casualty figures had not been anticipated by the War Office and those killed were in many instances buried in haste. This involved placing upended rifles in the ground to mark the graves, or given a simple cross with the deceased's name scrawled in chalk or even pencil which was easily washed away by weather conditions. Following the Battle of Waterloo a century earlier, the author William Makepeace Thackeray had commented that the bodies of those killed in action could no longer be *'shovelled into a hole…and so forgotten'* but opinions differed widely as to what should happen to the remains of the fallen, and how they should be commemorated.

As it happened, the Adjutant General of the BEF was Major General Sir Nevil McCready who had served in the Boer War, and he recalled the problems there resulting from attempting to record details of those killed in battle. So, when an energetic 45 year old Red Cross worker Fabian Ware (later Sir), arrived in France and began gathering evidence of British dead soldiers and how graves could be marked with a record taken of the exact location, McCready accepted his proposals. Consequently, Ware's work then became officially recognised and the Graves Registration Commission established in 1915, and incorporated into the British Army.

The subsequent need for a complete new organisation to care for graves after the war resulted in the constitution of the Imperial War Graves Commission by Royal Charter in 1917. The Prince of Wales became its first President with the Secretary of State for War, Lord Derby, as Chairman. Fabian Ware was appointed Vice-Chairman. Other Commissioners included the poet and author Rudyard Kipling who had lost a son in the war. Although the Commission was supposed to be as representative of every political view and social class as possible, no woman Commissioner was appointed. This is believed to be on account of most of the Commissioners being 'imbued with Victorian attitudes' that had no doubt been hardened by recollections of suffragette activities before the war. So the Commissioners failed to take note of the contribution women had made towards the war effort, and dismissed the thought that bereaved mothers had a right to help formulate policy. The Commission was charged with the responsibility for caring for the graves of all members of the Imperial Forces who 'died from wounds inflicted, accident occurring and disease contracted, while on active service, whether on sea or land'. It was also empowered to acquire and hold land for cemeteries, their maintenance, and the keeping of all necessary records.

When America entered the war, a promise was made by its government to return the bodies of the fallen to all relatives who wished to bury them near to their family homes. But their casualties were few, and the British Government had made no such commitment in relation to the British dead. In any event, when the fighting men themselves had been canvassed for their views after the Passchendaele offensive, they had expressed a unanimous and emphatic desire that those who fought and died together, officers and men, should be laid side by side in their final resting place facing the line they gave their lives to maintain. Consequently, the decision was made to create a so called 'fellowship of death' in the war cemeteries.

The decision, however, triggered fierce opposition from certain families at home who had lost loved ones in the conflict, resulting in the formation of a War Graves Appeal Committee which became active in canvassing MPs, etc. In 1919, approximately 90 letters were received weekly calling for repatriation of bodies and whilst the Commission was sympathetic, it remained adamant in refusal, confirming the 'fellowship of death' policy. Officials also firmly believed that repatriation would create a distinction between rich and poor, but the logistical consideration of moving the huge numbers of war dead across the world to their home countries was another real factor. What was generally not known to the bereaved families, however, was that the body of former Premier William Gladstone's grandson had been brought home from Poperinghe after 'pressure from a very high quarter'! Relatives also took exception to the principle of uniformity and the insistence of a headstone instead of a cross which they considered would resemble 'so many milestones'. In consequence, the Appeal Committee took advertising space in the press stating that the Commission had refused to allow bereaved families 'any say in regard to the graves of their loved ones'.

One local fervent campaigner for repatriation was Mrs Ruth Jervis of 'Kirkstone', Doxey in Stafford whose son, A/Bombardier Harry Jervis was killed in action during the Battle of Arras in April 1917. The wife of a railway signalman, she wrote a number of lengthy letters to the Commission making it expressly clear that she wished for her son's remains to be returned. *'The country took him'* she wrote, *'and the country should bring him back!'* [3] In another letter she wrote *'Militarism has destroyed his body and it seems to me that if some people in this country had the power they would deal with his soul also!'* She continued *'Thank heavens that at least, is beyond you!'* The grieving mother also took issue with the decision for 'uniform' military headstones as opposed to a cross which was the preference of many families. Noting that the inscription on the headstone should not exceed three lines - *'what next?'* she queried. *'Would the Commission seek to impose a condition as to how long we remain at the graveside when we get there?'* [4]

The Appeal Committee fought bravely on, holding mass meetings and petitioning for repatriation of the fallen. However, on 4th May 1920 Winston Churchill, by now Chairman of the Commission, successfully appealed to the House of Commons to confirm the Commission's proposal, after which the organisation was free to proceed unhindered with its work.

In spite of the standardisation and common architectural aims, it may be seen that each of the Commission's cemeteries has acquired a character of its own, often indicated by its name such as Sanctuary Wood, so recalled by the grim humour of those who fought there. Some even relate to former dressing stations. At the same time, the so called 'Silent Cities' represent the work of some of the most distinguished architects and sculptors of the generation including the likes of Sir Herbert Baker, Sir Edwin Lutyens and Sir Charles Wheeler. In 1960, the Commission became the Commonwealth War Graves Commission and today its work continues, extending worldwide from its headquarters in Maidenhead. Its vast operations are a long haul from its humble beginnings in 1914 when Fabian Ware began his work in France.

Notes

1 A. J. P. Taylor, *The First World War* (Penguin Books, 1966) p. 221.
2 Martin J. Farrar, *News from the Front* (Sutton Publishing, 1998) p. 207.
3 Letter to the Imperial War Graves Commission 1 Dec 1918.
4 *Ibid*, 21 Jan 1919.

An NCO of the Exhumation Squad at Work in Flanders
(Photo from the Imperial War Museum REF: Q100915)

King George V places First Wreath on the Cenotaph after the Unveiling,
11th November, 1919
(Postcard from Author's Collection)

TOWN HALL, CHEADLE.

GRAND

Victory Dance

ON

WEDNESDAY, NOV. 27TH, 1918,

7 p.m. to 11 p.m.

WALTZING COMPETITION

Prizes kindly given by
Mrs. MATHER.

For full details see large Bills.

PRICE TO DANCE 2/-.

Refreshments at Moderate Charges.

The whole of the Proceeds given to the
N.S. Prisoners of War Fund.

Poster of Victory Dance

15

EPILOGUE

The war of 1914-18 is often referred to as the Great War, whereas famously the author H.G. Wells called it *'The War that will end all War.'* To those who had fought in it and those who had lived through the period this may have become a common belief, and in doing so made the suffering seem more acceptable. But much of the detail of that suffering had, to a large extent, been withheld on the grounds of maintaining morale, etc. The terms of peace were finally concluded with the signing at Versailles on 28th June 1919 after which the Home Front would, hopefully, feel able to forget the war and the country look to the future. But they had not experienced the hell that was the Western Front - the mud, the smell of death and the incessant bombardment sometimes for weeks on end. They did not have to cope with the nightmare for the rest of their lives, as did so many of our ancestors. Thousands left the battlefields with their nerves shattered or suffering from the effects of gas, others having lost limbs and eyes. In any event, many of the soldiers of 1914-18 did not wish to talk about their experiences and what they had to endure. After all, how could anyone who had not witnessed the horrors of the Western Front and the resultant human suffering really understand? Their memories were too painful.

At the time of the signing of the Peace Treaty at Versailles, Muriel Masefield was on a short break in Malvern but no doubt still attempting to come to terms with the tragic loss of her beloved Charles. Together with 8 year old Geoff, she was staying at Rusland Lodge, the home of her mother. Later in life, Geoff recalled the occasion and *'the elation of the confirmation of the real peace and watching a wonderful celebratory torch light parade'* in the town. Having left Cheadle the year before the two were now living in Oxford, and it is from here-on-in that Muriel really began to reveal her full potential.

Having been earlier educated at Ealing's Princess Helena College, Muriel had won an exhibition to Lady Margaret Hall, Oxford but did not pursue this on becoming engaged to marry Charles. However, following his death, the young widow decided to continue with her studies, initially enrolling as a Home Student for the University's Diploma in Economics and Political Science. Having been successful in achieving the qualification, she subsequently converted it by additional studies and examinations gaining BA and MA degrees. At the time she was surviving on a small income and was experiencing problems relating to payment of a war widow's pension and gratuities. The situation was not helped by confusion arising from differing designations of her late husband's rank on various documents i.e. on some he remained as 2nd/Lt whereas at the time of his death he was Acting Captain! Writing from 3 Norham Road, Oxford some of her correspondence with War Office officials survives, and it appears that the matter took a period of 2 years before reaching a satisfactory conclusion. Naturally, this did not help in the predicament that she found herself in, seemingly identical to many other War Widows. Nevertheless, this extraordinary young woman built on her education achievements and obtained employment as an extension lecturer for Cambridge University, later gaining a similar position with Oxford University. In this capacity, she travelled to many provincial towns giving regular courses of lectures on economic topics, later extending these to include literature and social history. The author of a number of books in later life, she also undertook lecture tours in America. Amongst other activities, she was an enthusiastic supporter and Vice President of the Oxford Branch of the English Speaking Union. After a full and eventful life, Muriel Masefield died at Kidlington on 4th August 1973. She never remarried.

By the same token, her son was an achiever in a number of fields and a true polymath. Educated at the famous Dragon School, Oxford (where he was Head Boy) and Winchester College, he subsequently graduated with a 1st class Honours Degree in Botany at Balliol College. In later years on becoming a specialist in tropical agriculture, Dr Geoffrey Masefield was among the first to make a study of the prevention of famine and its relief. Having travelled extensively through his work and research, he was fluent in seven languages and had a smattering of a number of others.

The author of a number of books on various

aspects of tropical agriculture, Dr Masefield also published numerous research papers and articles in scientific journals. Also, following in his father's footsteps, he had two volumes of poetry published, together with books on local history which he wrote in retirement, although that word didn't appear to feature in his dictionary! A scientist by nature, he was also a countryman at heart, in particular retaining a love of the Staffordshire Moorlands from his childhood. He died in his 90th year on 2nd August 2001 and was survived by his wife Joy with whom he had three sons and a daughter. Geoffrey Masefield is said to have been *'personally unassuming'* and that *'he took great pride in the achievements of his wife and family.'* Having been raised as an only child, he remained *'extremely loyal to his mother, and intensely proud of his father.'*

The remains of Charles Masefield MC now lie in the dignified setting of the British Military Cemetery at Cabaret Rouge at Souchez, Pas de Calais. He lies with those other men who fought and died for the freedom we enjoy today. May we remain ever worthy of their sacrifice.

Muriel Masefield
(Photo Courtesy of Robin Masefield)

*Charles Masefield's Gravestone at the
Cabaret Rouge Military Cemetery
(Photo Courtesy of Michael Collis)*

*Memorial Window to Charles Masefield &
Cousins Aubrey Bowers & Homfray Addenbrooke,
Parish Church of St. Giles the Abbot, Cheadle
(Photograph taken by Lynne M. Bebbington, 2009)*

ABOUT THE AUTHOR

Photo taken by Lynne Bebbington (2013)

Graham Bebbington was born in 1938, the son of a blacksmith's striker in the mining village of Silverdale (i.e. a Daleian), although he has lived at Trentham since he married in 1973. He was educated at Silverdale County Primary School and Wolstanton County Grammar School.

He spent all his working life in the public service, firstly at West Midlands Gas Board. However, this employment was temporarily broken by National Service during 1957-9 when he joined the Royal Army Dental Corps attaining the rank of Corporal. He subsequently joined Newcastle Borough Council in 1964, culminating as Mayor's Secretary & Senior Committee Clerk. Prior to taking early retirement in 1993 he was appointed a fellow of the Institute of Administrative Management in recognition of 'distinction in the administrative service.'

Since leaving local government, he has dedicated the majority of his time to research and writing. A Member of the Society of Authors, he has had a number of books published, including *Pit Boy to Prime Minister* – the biography of Silverdale-born Australian Prime Minister Sir Joseph Cook. This was used in 1986 to launch Keele University's 'Staffordshire Heritage' series of publications.

In 2007, he was elected a Fellow of the Royal Historical Society. The fellowship is awarded to historians with a proven track record of published works or who have made a significant contribution to the knowledge and understanding of history by original research. It is approved by a Board of eminent academic scholars.

Great lovers of all types of music, he & his wife Lynne founded the Lavey Fund, a charity to support young musicians born in Staffordshire, and this is administered by Staffordshire Performing Arts.